GREAT VICTORIA DESERT

• Menzies

13

NULLARBOR PLAIN

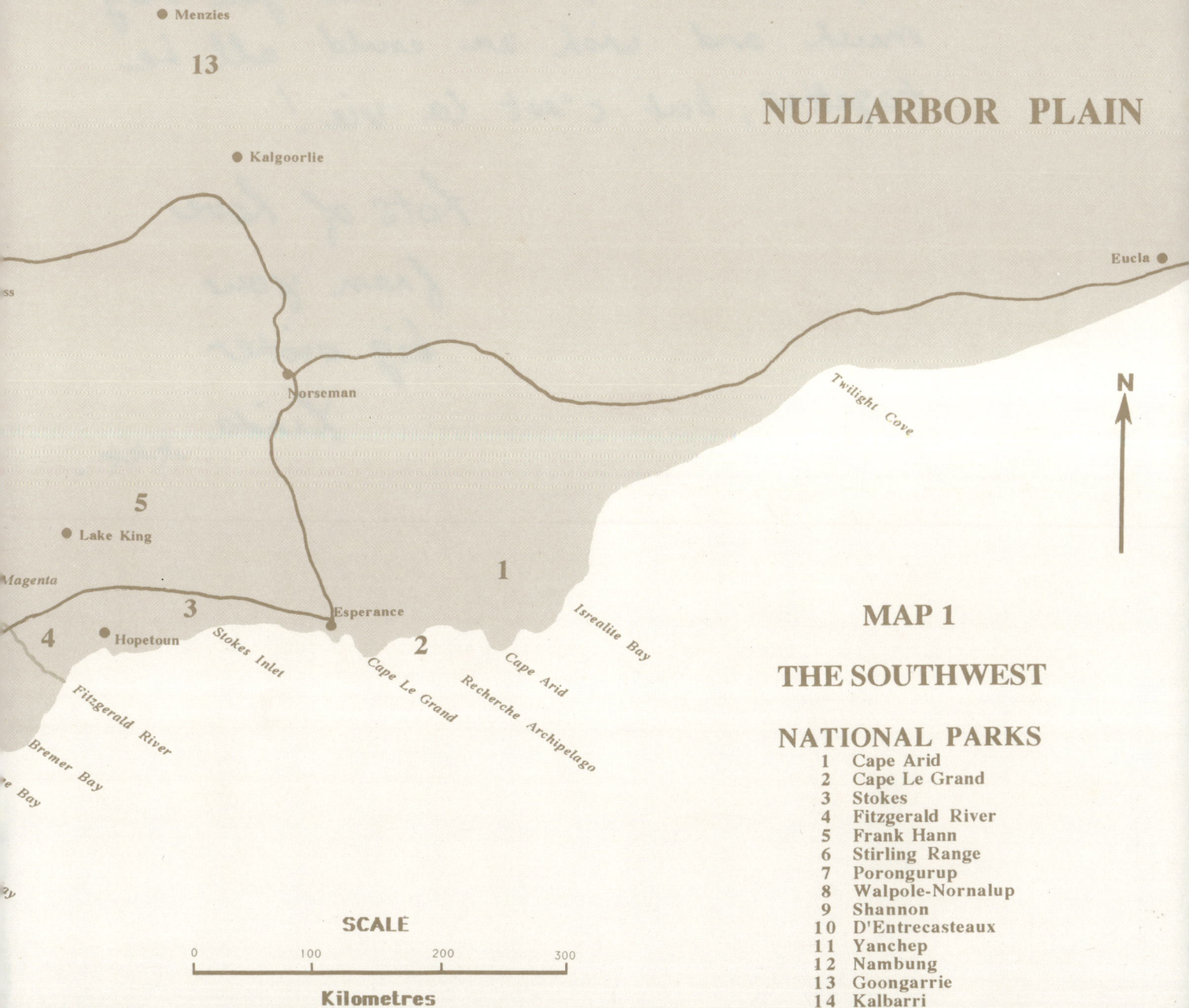

• Kalgoorlie

Eucla •

Norseman

*Twilight Cove*

**N**

5

• Lake King

1

Magenta

3

*Isrealite Bay*

4  • Hopetoun

Esperance

2

*Stokes Inlet*

*Cape Arid*

*Cape Le Grand*

*Recherche Archipelago*

*Fitzgerald River*

Bremer Bay

e Bay

y

MAP 1

THE SOUTHWEST

NATIONAL PARKS

1   Cape Arid
2   Cape Le Grand
3   Stokes
4   Fitzgerald River
5   Frank Hann
6   Stirling Range
7   Porongurup
8   Walpole-Nornalup
9   Shannon
10  D'Entrecasteaux
11  Yanchep
12  Nambung
13  Goongarrie
14  Kalbarri

SCALE

0          100         200         300

Kilometres

9th April 1994.

To Ramsay.

Hope this book will serve as a reminder of your holiday here (and of us), or will at least help to alleviate the boredom of the long trip home. I will miss you very much and wish we could all be together, but c'est la vie!

Lots of Love
from your
big sister
Linda xxx.

# THE
# LIVING WEST
# OF
# AUSTRALIA

# WESTERN AUSTRALIAN PRIMARY VEGETATION TYPES

**Northern Botanical Province**
*Tropical savanna and scrubland*

| | |
|---|---|
| **1** | High grass savanna woodland |
| **2** | Curly spinifex savanna woodland and tree savanna |
| **3** | Pindan (Acacia thicket with scattered trees) |
| **4** | Tall bunch grass savanna, with or without trees |
| **5** | Short bunch-grass savanna, with or without trees |
| **6** | Semi-desert spinifex steppe |

**South-West Botanical Province**

| | |
|---|---|
| **16** | Tall forest — Karri |
| **17** | Forest — Jarrah |
| **18** | Eucalypt woodlands — Tuart, marri, wandoo |
| **19** / **19/22** | " " — York gum and salmon gum |
| **20** / **20/22** | " " — Mixed dry woodlands |
| **21** | Banksia low woodland |
| **22** | Acacia-Casuarina thickets and scrub |
| **23** | Mallee |
| **24** | Mallee-heath |
| **25** | Scrub-heath |

**Eremaean Botanical Province**
*Desert grassland, low woodland and scrub*

| | |
|---|---|
| **7** | Tree and shrub steppe; spinifex with scattered eucalypts or shrubs |
| **8** | Desert oak; spinifex with groves of Casuarina |
| **9** | Mulga (Acacia aneura) low woodland and scrub |
| **10** | Other Acacia low woodland and scrub |
| **11** | Mulga parkland; spinifex steppe with patches of mulga |
| **12a** | Blue bush plains — Treeless |
| **12b** | " " — Lightly wooded |
| **12c** | " " — Thickly wooded |
| **13** | Halophytes; samphire and saltbush communities |
| **14** | Dwarf scrub of Cassia and Eremophila |
| **15** | Intermediate sandplains; mixed spinifex and heath |
| | Playa lakes, mainly bare mud and salt |

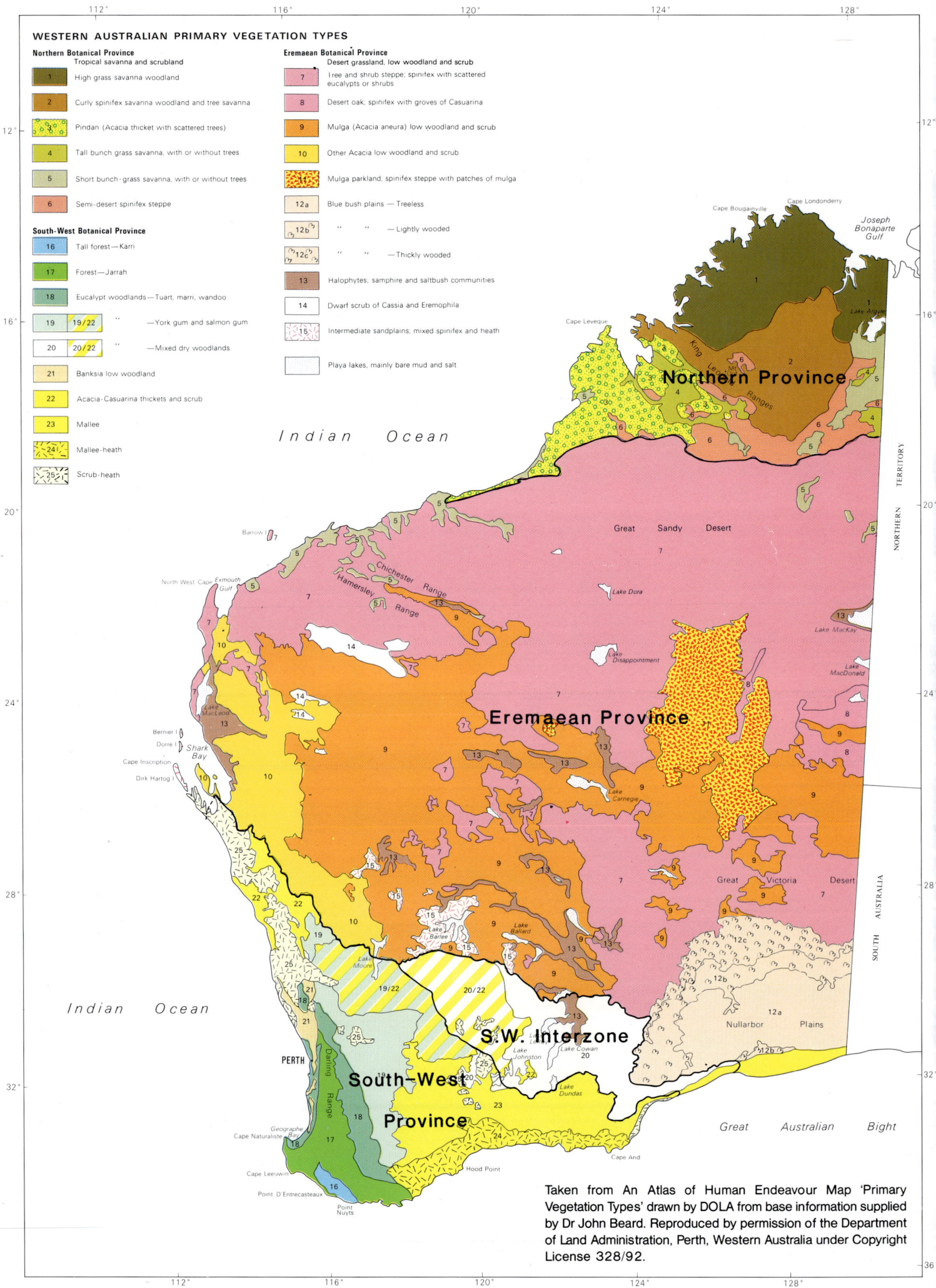

*Indian Ocean*

**Northern Province**

*Indian Ocean*

**Eremaean Province**

**S.W. Interzone**

**South-West Province**

*Great Sandy Desert*

*Great Victoria Desert*

*Nullarbor Plains*

*Great Australian Bight*

PERTH

Cape Bougainville · Cape Londonderry · Joseph Bonaparte Gulf · Lake Argyle · King Leopold Ranges · Cape Leveque · Barrow I. · North West Cape · Exmouth Gulf · Hamersley Range · Chichester Range · Lake Dora · Lake MacKay · Lake Disappointment · Lake MacDonald · Lake MacLeod · Bernier I. · Dorre I. · Shark Bay · Cape Inscription · Dirk Hartog I. · Lake Carnegie · Lake Ballard · Lake Barlee · Lake Moore · Lake Johnston · Lake Cowan · Lake Dundas · Darling Range · Geographe Bay · Cape Naturaliste · Cape Leeuwin · Point D'Entrecasteaux · Point Nuyts · Hood Point · Cape Arid · NORTHERN TERRITORY · SOUTH AUSTRALIA

# THE LIVING WEST OF AUSTRALIA

### JAN TAYLOR

Kangaroo Press

# PREFACE

This book follows the excellent lead given by Alec Blombery with his book *The Living Centre of Australia*. The aim is to provide a book which concisely introduces and illustrates all facets of the natural environment for people interested in the countryside. The scope extends from the geology and landforms to the vegetation, plants, mammals, birds and other fauna found in the area. Western Australia is a larger area than covered in Blombery's book and has a more diverse climatic range, and hence a more varied flora and fauna, which is reflected in the extended coverage of these sections. Other groups have had to be omitted such as the fungi, lichens and most of the invertebrate fauna.

The flora of Western Australia is virtually unrivaled in its diversity, so it is hard to do it justice in such a short book. Accurately identifying plants is not easy for the layperson let alone the specialist, and the grouping of plants by such methods as the colour of the flower, or growth form, although superficially making identification appear easy, are only of value when describing plants in a small area, such as Kings Park. When covering the State as a whole, there may be dozens or even hundreds of plants which could answer a superficial description. These methods also do not help people to become acquainted with the fascinating variety of flower structures which distinguish the various plant families. It is my view that it is much better, and more instructive to learn to distinguish the different families and genera of plants, and to be able to say with some authority that a plant is in the Buttercup Family, or that another is a kind of *Grevillea*, than to try for species names when in Western Australia there may be so many plants which can only be distinguished by using botanical keys. With this in mind I have chosen to illustrate as many families and important genera as the space allows. The fauna section has been approached in a similar way, providing examples of the most important groups.

The numbers of species given are necessarily approximate, because taxonomy is an active science, and new species are being added and revisions are constantly under way. In this regard it may be helpful to add something on what constitutes a species. We know that all people, apart from identical twins have a unique genetic make up, but some people are more similar than others. The same applies in plants and animals, all of which are constantly changing with the process of evolution. Each type may have considerable variations over its geographic range, but it is the province of the taxonomist to decide where one species ends and another begins. In animals this can often be determined if it can be shown that no successful interbreeding occurs, even when they live in the same place the genes of one species do not find their way into the other: thus the two white-tailed black-cockatoos are distinct species. However this is expensive and time-consuming work, and many firm species remain lumped together, awaiting analysis, particularly in the insect world, where species more different than chimpanzees and man are still put together, because we do not see the differences, but which are presumably obvious to the insects themselves. Species boundaries are harder to determine in plants, because they are much less mobile than animals, and have great genetic differences and little or no gene flow, such as in the Rock Isotome which is found growing on rock stacks isolated from one another. Here species are often determined by degree of difference, distribution and constancy of form. This approach leads to divisions between taxonomists the 'splitters' who give species status to forms which are described as varieties or sub-species by the 'lumpers'. The difficulty is compounded by plants using animals to disperse pollen and having a greater ability to form crosses, thus kangaroo paws readily form crosses if brought close to one another. This frequently happens when the natural distributions are disturbed by human activity similar happenings occur in some animals, such as the duck family, where most duck species will produce crosses if caged together. Some will even do so in city lakes such as between the Mallard and Black Duck.

This book covers the whole state of Western Australia, but gives less prominence to the Kimberley Region, because at a later stage it is intended to produce another volume *The Living North of Australia* which will cover this area in more detail.

Over the years I have received considerable botanical guidance from Dr Arthur Weston. He kindly looked through my slides and put me right on some determinations and nomenclature. He has also contributed some excellent slides from his expeditions to the Kimberley Region (on pages 16, 17 & 19). I am also indebted to Ross for the photograph of a Doublebar Finch on page 78. I thank Dr John Beard and the Dept of Land Administration for permission to reproduce his vegetation map of Western Australia. Finally, I thank Madeleine for continuing to bear with my full-time occupation while she keeps the wolf from the door, and for helping with syntax and proof-reading.

JAN TAYLOR, *July 1992*

*© Jan Taylor 1992*

*First published in 1992 by Kangaroo Press Pty Ltd*
*3 Whitehall Road (P.O. Box 75)*
*Kenthurst NSW 2156*
*Printed in Hong Kong by Colorcraft Ltd*

Taylor, Jan (Jan C.).
The living west of Australia.

Bibliography.
Includes index.
ISBN 0 86417 434 9.

1. Botany – Western Australia. 2. Zoology – Western Australia.
I. Title.

574.9941

# CONTENTS

# PHYSICAL ENVIRONMENT

The state of Western Australia occupies the western third of the continent with longitude 129°E marking the boundary with South Australia and the Northern Territory. It covers an area of about 2.5 million square km, which, for comparison, is over a quarter of the size of the United States, 20 times the size of England, or an area greater than that of western Europe. It is located between the latitudes 13° 44'S and 35° 08'S with the tropic of Capricorn running through the Pilbara region and striking the coast near Coral Bay. From the south coast it is about 2500 km to Antarctica and from the north about 450 km to the nearest islands in Indonesia. It is over 5000 km from Africa, but shares many similarities with the area extending from Tanzania to the Cape.

## Climate

The major deserts of the world are found around the tropics of Cancer and Capricorn, where air rising by convection over the equator falls back to earth. The climate of Western Australia is dominated by this feature, and with no mountain chains to complicate the pattern most of the state is classified as either arid or semi-arid. Nevertheless the country extends from temperate to tropical regions and inevitably experiences a wide range of climatic conditions. Weather patterns in the lower southern hemisphere generally gyrate around the Antarctic in an easterly direction, hence Western Australia experiences a succession of high and low pressure systems coming from the west. High pressure systems (anticyclones) have air circulating in an anti-clockwise direc-

tion and bring dry weather, while lows have clockwise winds and bring rain. (It is interesting to note that the direction of circulation is opposite to that found in the northern hemisphere.) A dry, anticyclonic belt which occurs across the continent brings Mediterranean conditions to southern parts.

In summer (December-February) the weather patterns are shifted to the south so that equatorial monsoonal conditions approach the Kimberley region, bringing heavy rainfall, particularly to coastal areas. Summer rain also occurs in the Pilbara region, usually from convective thunderstorms. The band of arid climate moves south to affect the southern half of the state which has hot, dry summers.

In winter the weather patterns move north so that the Kimberley and Pilbara experience drought and the south-west receives some of the weather normally found in the temperate, roaring forties, well south of the continent. Cold fronts associated with low pressure bring rain to the south-west corner, with rainfall tailing off at the northern end of the fronts and as they pass inland. Annual rainfall in the Kimberley ranges from 250 to 1000 mm, in the Pilbara it is 200-300 mm and in the south 200-1500 mm, with most occurring in the populated south-west corner. The inland desert regions, which comprise most of Western Australia, are characterised by long periods of drought with occasional, unreliable rainfall.

**Sunset at Cape Arid** *(LEFT)*
**Frost on a sundew plant** *(BELOW)*
**Yallingup Cave** *(OPPOSITE)*

**Iron ore mining near Newman** *(LEFT)*
**The Pinnacles** *(ABOVE)*
**The Basin, Rottnest Island** *(OPPOSITE)*

Most of the country experiences high summer temperatures with maxima over 40°C common in the north. Although temperatures are high, the air is usually dry, and the heat less oppressive than in more humid parts of the world. Marble Bar has recorded temperatures over 40°C on 70 consecutive days and is regarded as the hottest place in Australia. Gascoyne Junction has recorded 50°C and many desert areas away from weather stations may experience similar temperatures.

Winter temperatures are pleasant in the north with Broome, for example, having a lowest monthly average maximum of about 28°C. The south becomes cool with maxima in the order of 18°C during the coolest month. Night frosts may occur in most inland areas, including the north, and snow occasionally falls on the Stirling Range.

The area experiences some severe weather events which affect the landscape. They may be sudden and devastating like the cyclones (known as hurricanes or typhoons in other parts of the world) which mainly strike the north-west. These appear most summers and usually cut a narrow path across the country in a south-easterly direction. They strafe the land with 200 km/hr winds, and heavy rain may cause serious flooding. Cyclone Alby reached the south-west in 1978 and caused widespread fire damage. Other weather phenomena may be protracted, such as long-term drought. Reliable rainfall is not a feature of the climate, so drought is normal, but it becomes devastating when protracted over a period of years. Huge fires burn for months on end in the Kimberley during serious droughts, mulga dies and mass emu migrations occur during droughts in the Murchison River area, and wheat farmers become bankrupt when drought strikes areas in the south-west.

## Geology

Western Australia has very ancient rock formations including some of the oldest known minerals (4.4 billion years old), oldest rocks (3.8 billion years old) and oldest fossils (3.5 billion years old). The major part of the south-west is made up of the very ancient Yilgarn Block of igneous rocks which include gold-bearing greenstone belts. Further north in the Pilbara there are old sedimentary rocks where iron ore is found. The iron was probably deposited by bacterial action between 2.5 and 1.8 billion years ago, before oxygen was present in the atmosphere. The Kimberley region possesses an extensive area of fossil Devonian coral reef, while the west coast and central desert regions have sedimentary deposits formed when the sea invaded these areas. Permian fossil shells can be found in the Gascoyne, Cretaceous ammonites near Gingin, Tertiary fossils in limestone forming the Nullarbor Plain and Pleistocene limestone near Perth dating from the last ice age.

Surface features include large areas of laterite and other capstones which form in areas subject to alternating rain and drought. It is thought that deep-weathering rocks break down into dissolved and colloidal material which, during times of drought, is drawn to the surface to form a solidified crust. Below-ground capstones and limestone hardened around roots are often exposed by wind near the coast. The best example can be seen at the Pinnacles Desert north of Perth. Solution processes have produced impressive limestone caves in the south-west, Cape Range and Nullarbor. Many arid areas have stabilized sand ridges dating back to the last ice age when the country experienced severe drought and high winds, especially in the north-west from Kalbarri to Onslow, and in the Great Sandy, Gibson and Great Victoria Deserts. Other features include large areas of salt lake following the paths of ancient river systems, some dating back to the time when Australia had a temperate climate and was covered by southern beech or pine forests.

Other geological features of interest include the well-known meteorite crater at Wolf Creek in the Kimberley, which is 850 m across and dates from about 25 million years ago. Others up to 28 km diameter have been identified. The most accessible one, Dalgaranga near Mt Magnet, is 21 m across and was formed 26 000 years ago. The Nullarbor region has proved to be one of the most productive areas in the world for finding meteorites, which are lumps of rock or metal originating from the Asteroids. Some are thought to come from the Moon or Mars, having been thrown up by the impact of an asteroid. Other finds of extra-terrestrial origin include bead-like stones of black glass known as tektites, believed to have been formed when asteroids hit the earth. Large numbers have been found scattered across southern Australia, particularly in the Kalgoorlie area. They date from an event about 700 000 years ago, but the site of the asteroid impact, if that is what formed them, is not known.

Up until 1968 Western Australia was generally thought of as a very stable land mass, not subject to earthquake activity. This view was revised after the Meckering earthquake on 14 October of that year, which severely damaged the small wheatbelt town, shook Perth over 100 km away and built a 37 km long ridge along a faultline cutting across the main highway. Since then other earthquakes have rocked the state, especially one centred at Calingiri. More serious earthquakes may have occurred in the past. This is suggested by an abrupt change in sea level identified at Rottnest Island, and dated at 4800 years ago, when the island probably rose by over two metres.

# Geographical Features

IT MAY BE BEST to divide the country into three parts: (1) the South-west comprising all the country south of a line through Geraldton, including Kalgoorlie and the Nullarbor Plain; (2) the North-west to include the Pilbara and country north of the line; and (3) the Kimberley, which extends from Broome to the Northern Territory border.

## The South-west

The region is mainly made up of a large undulating plateau between about 200 and 500 metres high. The Darling Scarp or Range marks the western edge of the plateau, where the land surface drops to a 30 km wide coastal plain, which stretches along the west and south coasts. The continental shelf extends a further 30 km beyond Rottnest Island into the Indian Ocean.

### RANGES
### Darling Range

This is better termed the Darling Scarp, because it is the western edge of the continental plateau rather than a free-standing range of hills. It is formed mainly of dissected old granitic rocks and extends from Moora to Donnybrook with Mt Dale being one of the highest points at 546 m. Much of the rock surface has been weathered to a depth of 20-30 metres and is covered in a layer of laterite (known as bauxite when it contains high concentrations of aluminium) which forms a hard cap. The hills often have flat tops of rock which break away at the edges, a formation known locally as a *breakaway*. Bauxite forms the basis of large-scale mining operations to extract alumina, particularly at Jarrahdale and Boddington. The latter site also contains gold, and this mine is one of the main gold producers in Australia. The laterite has also been used in the past as a source of iron ore, but has been superseded by the richer ore deposits in the Pilbara.

### Stirling Range

This outstanding range of hills north of Albany can be seen from over 100 km away. The ridge runs on an east-west axis with a number of peaks. At the eastern end the highest points include Ellen Peak, Isongerup Peak and Bluff Knoll which at 1073 m is the highest point in the Range. In the middle there are the popular climbs of Mt Trio, Mt Hassell and Toolbrunup Peak. Other hills can be seen along the scenic Stirling Drive which runs through the national park. This is the highest range in the south-west, and is made of very old sedimentary rocks which were laid down in a shallow sea. Ripple marks left in the sand well over a billion years ago can readily be seen fossilized in rocks near the summits. Earth movements associated with the formation of the south coast granites probably compacted the sediments into hard, mountain-forming rocks.

### Porongurup Range

This picturesque range of granite hills between the Stirling Range and Albany originated about the same time as most of the granite outcrops found along the south coast, from Cape Arid to beyond Walpole. The formation of the granite was probably associated with the turbulent events in the Earth's crust which eventually produced the rift that separated Australia from Antarctica. The hills are bare, rounded, rocky outcrops covered in lichens and moss, with Devil's Slide forming the highest point at 670 m. Near the base of the rock grow patches of Karri trees, isolated from the main Karri forest area which stretches along the south coast from Pemberton. Much of the forest in the Porongurup Range has been cut down or killed by fires, but is being replaced by a strong regrowth of young trees. In recent years the area near the range has proved to be one of the best for producing high quality wines.

### The Barrens

These attractive hills are in the Fitzgerald River National Park between Hopetoun and Bremer Bay, east of Albany. They include the Whoogarup Range, Annie Peak, and the East, Mid and West Mt Barrens. They were formed by a process similar to that of the Stirling Range, but the rocks are more highly metamorphosed. East Mt Barren, which is accessible by road, is composed of a hard, white quartzite rock. Unfortunately restrictions have had to be imposed on climbing the hills, because die-back disease is destroying the unique flora of the area and can be spread further by walkers carrying spores on their shoes.

**Avon Gorge at Walyunga National Park in the Darling Range** *(LEFT)*
**View of Bluff Knoll from Toolbrunup Peak in the Stirling Range** *(BELOW)*

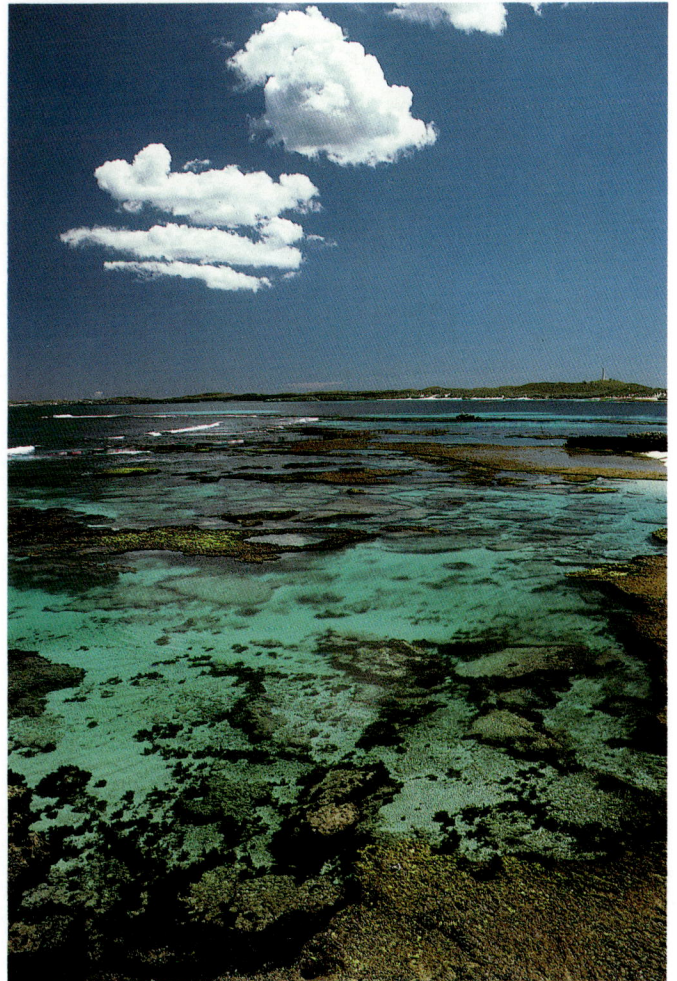

**Salmon Point, Rottnest Island** *(ABOVE)*
**Mt Trio from Mt Hassell in the Stirling Range** *(LEFT)*

## COASTAL SCENERY AND ISLES
### West Coast

Much of the west coast is bounded by limestone ridges, reefs and sand dunes, with the shore open to the Indian Ocean swell. The treacherous coastline was used by early Dutch sailors to navigate their way to Batavia, and the islands near Geraldton were given the meaningful name of Abrolhos (watch out!). Sailors on several vessels failed to hear the breakers in time, and their ships were wrecked along the coast, including the Batavia in 1629 and the Vergulden Draeck in 1656. The limestone dates from the last ice age when sea levels were up to 150 m lower than they are at present. Strong winds at that time swept abundant shell-sand from the exposed sea bed into tall dunes. Since their formation, the action of rain has turned the dunes into limestone. This rock is particularly well represented on Rottnest Island, where the layers within the original sand dunes are clearly visible in the cliffs. Some of the limestone dates from prior to the last ice age when sea levels were higher than they are at present. These rocks contain fossil corals, including kinds which are only found as far south as the Abrolhos Islands now. This means that the sea must have been warmer around Rottnest then.

Other islands include Garden Island off Rockingham, which is now a naval base, and Penguin Island in Safety Bay. Further south an attractive stretch of coastline can be found between Busselton and Augusta, where a ridge of granite separated from the Darling Range runs along the coast, and which includes areas of deep limestone with extensive cave systems. Some of the best surf is to be found near Margaret River and Yallingup.
### South Coast

The coastal scenery here includes some of the best in Australia. It is studded with granite outcrops and extends into the Recherche Archipelago, which is a swarm of granite islands off Esperance. There are also patches of coastal limestone, sand dunes and at Black Point an exposure of columnar basalt, similar to that forming the Giant's Causeway in Ireland. Particularly attractive places include William Bay near Denmark, King George Sound at Albany, Two People's Bay, Cheyne Bay, Bremer Bay, bays in the Fitzgerald River National Park, Esperance, Cape Le Grand National Park and Cape Arid National Park. Coastal fishing can be treacherous with large waves, known as king waves, sometimes overturning boats and sweeping people off rocks. However, there are also many inlets cut off from the sea, such as the Broke, Nornalup and Stokes Inlets, which are ideal for boating enthusiasts and recreational fishermen.

## INLAND PLAINS

The inland area is mainly made up of gently undulating countryside with high points formed from granite outcrops, such as at Wave Rock, near Hyden, or various other hard rocks, such as the gold-bearing greenstone, or quartz veins. Low points have loamy soils with salmon gums, or may have extensive salt lake systems, such as at Lake Grace. Many areas have important mineral deposits, especially gold and nickel in the Kalgoorlie-Norseman region.

The Nullarbor Plain extends east of the Goldfields into South Australia. It was formed when land movements brought the sea across central Australia, where it deposited a deep layer of

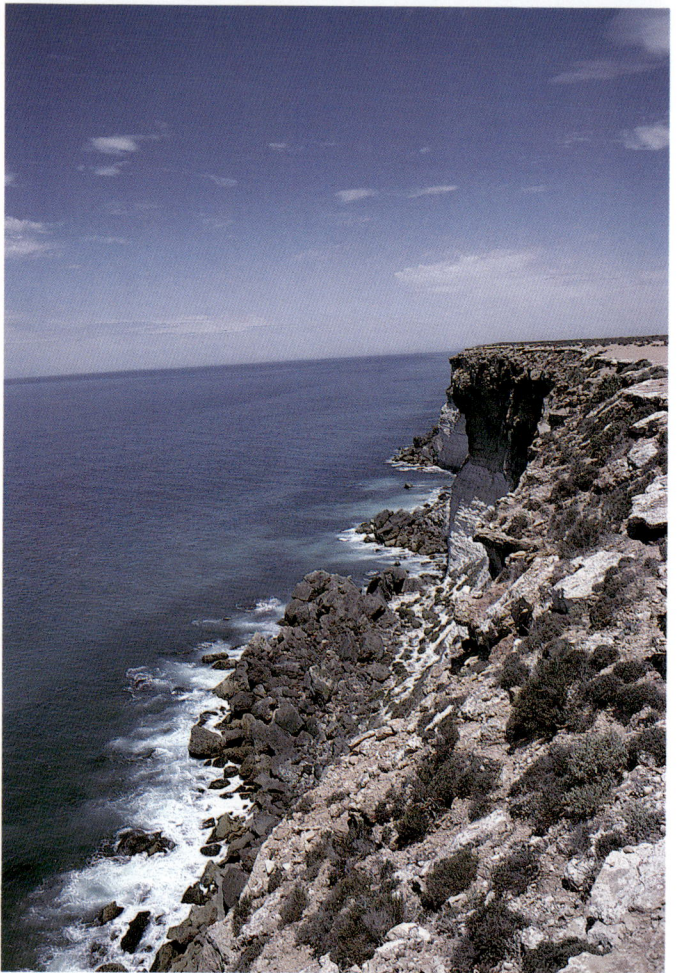

**Columnar basalt rock at Black Point, D'Entrecasteaux National Park** *(TOP LEFT)*
**Lucky Bay, Cape Le Grand National Park** *(TOP RIGHT)*
**Marram Grass on a sand dune at Stokes National Park** *(ABOVE)*
**Cliffs at the edge of the Nullarbor Plain** *(ABOVE RIGHT)*

limestone. Later movements brought the land above water again to form the plain. The edge has been worn away by the sea to form a long line of cliffs, but further land movement has resulted in a section of the cliffs ending up high and dry inland between Twilight Cove and Eucla.

## LAKES AND RIVERS

With high rainfall concentrated within the few winter months, water collects into many lakes and rivers in the south-west corner of the state. The early explorers Vlamingh and Captain Stirling were impressed by the large tidal inlet they found. It was named the Swan River, because there were black swans there. Further inland another river was found stretching through York and Northam, which was called the Avon. Only later was it realized that it was all part of the same system, cutting through the Darling Range in a deep gorge. In those days the water was fresh in the river and the estuary was also less saline. Land clearance for farming has made the water highly saline in summer, while the estuary has been opened to the sea by blasting the bar across the river mouth at Fremantle. Efforts are being made to keep salt out of the other rivers by replanting trees and controlling land clearance, partly so that the water can be used to supply dams and reservoirs. The main rivers going south from Perth are the Murray, which like the Swan River has a large tidal inlet at Mandurah, the Collie, Blackwood, Donnelly, Warren and Frankland Rivers. Other rivers further east along the south coast such as the Fitzgerald River are often salty and have intermittent flows, occasionally flooding.

The west coastal plain, being flat and made up of sand and limestone, has many lakes and swamps much used by waterbirds. Most are freshwater, but Lakes Clifton and Preston near Bunbury and those on Rottnest Island are salt. Inland Lakes are mostly salt, and frequently dry. They include Lake Dumbleyung where Donald Campbell broke the water speed record in 1964, Lakes Grace, King and Magenta in the south, Mongers Lake and Lake Moore inland from Geraldton near Dalwallinu, and others in the Southern Cross-Kalgoorlie area.

## The North-west

This is a huge area of arid and semi-arid land stretching from Geraldton to Broome and across to the state border near Giles. It extends into the Great Sandy, Gibson and Victoria Deserts which have more affinity with the region described in Alec Blombery's book *The Living Centre of Australia*. Like the south-west, it is mainly made up of an ancient undulating land surface, mainly over 500 m above sea level and without any high mountains.

### RANGES
Although lacking high mountains, the region contains a number of attractive ranges.
### Hamersley Range
This is the most spectacular range in the region. It includes Mt Meharry (1251 m) and Mt Bruce (1235 m) which are the highest

**Hamersley Range** (BELOW)
**Salt-encrusted pools in the Fitzgerald River** (RIGHT)
**Lake Grace** (BOTTOM)

points in Western Australia. The range is largely made up of banded iron formations which contain pockets of iron ore, being mined at several sites, especially at Newman, Tom Price and Paraburdoo. It also contains areas of granite and has deep gorges, valleys and steep slopes covered in spinifex grass and snappy gums.
### Chichester Range
This range is between the Hamersley Range and the coast. It is an area of contrasts and startling colours, and is characterised by block-like ancient greenstone volcanic rocks, which weather into a bright rusty-red colour. The hills also include banded iron formations and areas of granite. The rocks continue to the coast and extend along the Burrup Peninsula near Karratha.
### Cape Range
Found along the extreme north-west corner near Exmouth, the backbone of this range has relatively recent origins. The rocks were deposited in the sea about 30 million years ago and are still rising due to earth movements. Limestone in the range provides suitable conditions for cave formation, and caves in the area have been found to contain many interesting troglodytes, including blind fish. The geological structure is also conducive to the collection of oil deposits and drilling has been conducted in the area. However the main finds have been to the north in the sea around Barrow Island.
### Kennedy Range
This range consists of a colourful, cliff-like scarp running north from Gascoyne Junction with a sand ridge-covered plateau on top. The rocks which make up the range are very rich in fossil remains. These consist mainly of marine organisms, but petrified wood is also present in the area. The deposits date from the Permian period about 240 million years ago, when there were ice ages, and pine forests covered Australia.
### Mt Augustus
In many respects this mountain rivals Ayers Rock, being much larger and higher. It rises to 1105 m from a plain in a very remote area, and is composed of a single block of very old quartzite conglomerate rock — some claim it is the largest rock in the world.

**Greenstone on the Burrup Peninsula** *(LEFT)*
**The Fortescue River at Gregory Gorge in the Chichester Range** *(ABOVE)*

## Other Hills

One of the features of the region is flat-topped hills rising above the plain. They usually have steep sides where the rock erodes and breaks away. They represent the remains of an old land surface, which was once an extensive plain. It was uplifted by land movements and subsequently eroded away, leaving only these hills which are protected by hard caps of rock. This sort of a hill is known as a mesa.

## SAND RIDGES

As mentioned above these are found across extensive areas in this region. At present they are stable, with a cover of vegetation, but may become active again when the next ice age arrives. They are mainly aligned in northwest-southeast or east-west directions and some ridges may extend for hundreds of kilometres without a break. They have an abundant wildlife associated with them, because they represent one of the most widespread ecosystems in Australia. Coastal areas have dunes which are still active, such as those near Coral Bay.

## GORGES

Some of the most spectacular scenery is to be found in the gorges, where crystal-clear pools, shady trees and towering cliffs form welcome breaks in this otherwise stark landscape. The Hamersley Range gorges are particularly attractive, cutting through the deep-red banded iron formations. Some of the best known are Dales, Knox, and Wittenoom Gorges. Other gorges in the region are present in the Cape Range and Kalbarri National Parks. Kalbarri is where the Murchison River cuts through old sandstone hills just north of Geraldton. Fossil sea scorpion tracks can be seen in flat rock surfaces.

## COASTAL SCENERY

The coast from Geraldton to Broome has a number of interesting features. From Kalbarri north there is a long line of cliffs running to Useless Loop on the Shark Bay Peninsula. These are known as the Zuydorp Cliffs because a Dutch East India ship of that name was wrecked on this treacherous coast. In Shark Bay itself there is a large area of protected waters where dugongs are plentiful, and dolphins visit swimmers at Monkey Mia. At the southern tip in Hamelin Pool there are living examples of stromatolites. These structures are built by bacteria known as cyanobacteria or blue-green algae, and were only known as ancient fossils until discovered here. Many others have now been found, including some at Lake Clifton and in the lakes on Rottnest Island. Large waves strike the coast at the Blowholes north of Carnarvon where underwater caves trap air and spray is blown through cracks in the rock.

Further up the coast the shore is protected by Ningaloo Reef. This is an outstanding coral reef, rivalling the Great Barrier Reef in the diversity of life it supports. It extends to the tip of the Cape and in places comes close enough inshore for visitors to wade out to it through the lagoon. Exmouth Gulf is another shallow protected area where there is an important prawn fishery. The eastern side is largely inaccessible and has extensive mangrove swamps. Patches of mangrove extend along much of the northern coast together with open sand, especially along the Eighty Mile Beach, south of Broome.

Islands along the coast include Bernier and Dorre north of Shark Bay and Barrow Island off Onslow. These islands are very important reserves, because they have remaining populations of some of Australia's rarest marsupials. These animals have survived because there are no foxes, cats, stock or rabbits present.

## LAKES AND RIVERS

The northern rivers mostly have large catchment areas and flood after torrential rain, particularly when cyclones pass through the area in summer. The Murchison River catchment extends well beyond Meekatharra and the Geraldton-Carnarvon highway used to be frequently cut at Galena by flooding until a high bridge was constructed. The river runs out to sea through the Kalbarri Gorge.

The Gascoyne River extends beyond Mt Augustus where there are attractive permanent pools on the Lyons River. The river supplies water for the banana crop at Carnarvon, where flooding sometimes occurs.

The Ashburton River rises as far away as Newman, near where the Fortescue River also rises. The latter is a particularly attractive river, having many tree-lined billabongs and flower-covered floodplains. It runs between the Hamersley and Chichester ranges through an area of land with artesian water. Springs emerge from the underlying dolomite rock to feed streams and deep river pools at Millstream. This area has the feeling of an oasis in the desert, with large areas of palm trees and lush vegetation. After Millstream the river cuts through the Chichester Range at Gregory Gorge where a dam may be built to supply water to the town of Karratha.

The last river in this area is the De Grey which extends towards the Great Sandy Desert from near Port Hedland.

# The Kimberley District

This region extends from Broome to Kununurra and the state boundary. It includes the towns of Derby, Fitzroy Crossing, Halls Creek and Wyndham and extends south to the borders of the

Great Sandy and Tanami Deserts. Like the rest of the state, much of the region is an undulating plateau between 200 and 500 m high. There are often cliffs at the edge where rivers carve scenic gorges and cascade down waterfalls. The geology of the area is of great interest and includes valuable diamond-bearing kimberlite pipes. One of the best fossilized Devonian coral reefs known can be seen at Windjana Gorge, and fossilized dinosaur footprints are present in the rocks at Broome. South of Halls Creek there is the Wolf Creek meteorite crater, which is nearly a kilometre in diameter.

The Kimberley district includes large areas of wilderness and dramatic scenery deserving World Heritage listing, but is largely inaccessible to tourists.

**Living stromatolites at Hamelin Pool, Shark Bay** (TOP)
**Knox Gorge in the Hamersley Range National Park** (LEFT)
**Ashburton River** (ABOVE)

## RANGES

The highest points in the region are found in the King Leopold Range, which approach 1000 m above sea level. This is east of the Napier Range, which is cut by Windjana Gorge. Other ranges include the Carr Boyd and Ragged Ranges on the west side of Lake Argyle, and the Blatchford Escarpment to the south. Ragged Range has an extraordinary dome-like hill in it. Like the Pilbara region, the area is generally characterised by many attractive flat-topped hills, which are the remnants of an old land surface.

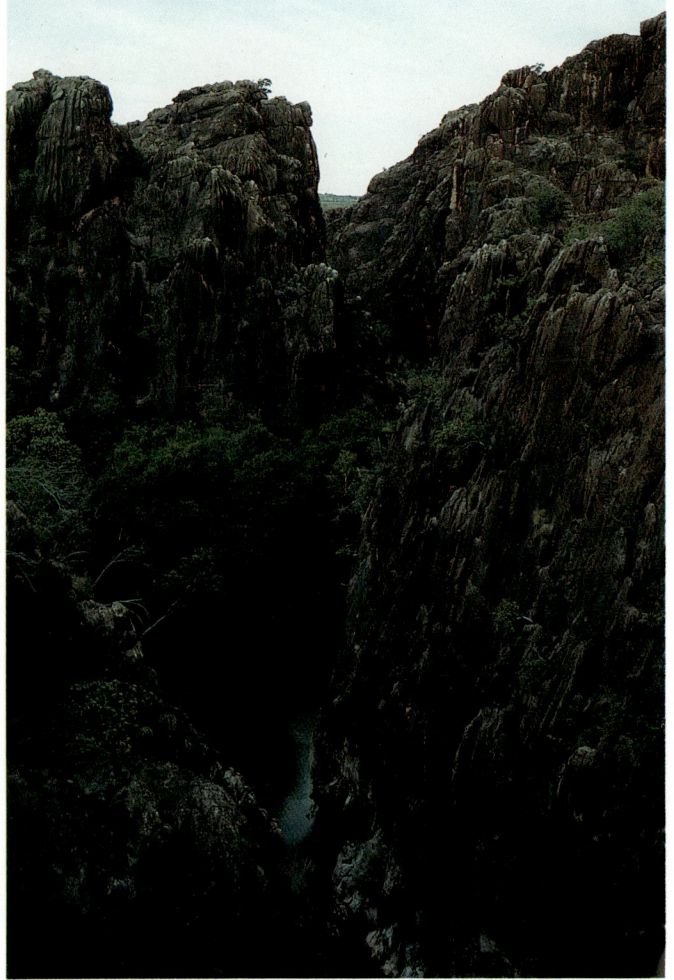

The Bungle Bungle Range south of Kununurra is a unique area which catches the imagination. It is situated in one of the more arid parts of the region and has weathered into strangely sculptured conglomerate domes, reminiscent of ancient Hindu temples. The rock surface is very fragile, and has to be protected from the tread of heavy feet — both human and of feral donkeys.

## GORGES

Spectacular gorges are to be found in the region. The best known are Windjana, Geiki and Tunnel Creek, however there are many others in the region, including Bells Gorge in the King Leopold Range. At Windjana the evocative nature of this cathedral-like gorge is enhanced by flocks of corellas, Aboriginal rock art and fossil traces of the life that once teamed around long-dead coral reefs.

## RIVERS

The Ord is a large river which was dammed in 1972 to produce Lake Argyle — the largest freshwater body in Western Australia. The lake is used to supply water for irrigation, and considerable

**Fortescue River near the Fortescue River Roadhouse**
*(OPPOSITE TOP LEFT)*
**Upper reaches of the Fortescue River near Newman after
heavy rain** *(OPPOSITE TOP RIGHT)*
**Bungle Bungle** *A.S. WESTON (OPPOSITE BOTTOM)*
**In the Napier Range** *A.S. WESTON (ABOVE LEFT)*
**Livistona palms in Bungle Bungle** *A.S. WESTON (ABOVE)*

work has had to be done to reduce the rate of silting, because much of the catchment area had been denuded by years of overgrazing. Stock was removed, and the area revegetated to bind the soil and reduce the rate at which it was being washed into the lake.

The Drysdale River runs through the large and remote Drysdale River National Park. The Prince Regent River, well-known for the King Cascades, follows a geological feature in a straight north-west line to the sea. The Mitchell River drains the Mitchell Plateau area and also has spectacular waterfalls. The large Fitzroy River enters the sea near Derby and drains the inland area including Geiki Gorge and Halls Creek.

# *Access*

TRAVEL IN WESTERN AUSTRALIA is mainly by road or air, with public transport available to all major centres. The main road links are all sealed and in good condition especially in the south-west, and the final section of Highway 1 in the Kimberley has been completed. Other roads are variable and drivers need to consult up-to-date maps for details. Off the main roads the surface is often gravel and drivers have to exercise caution, avoiding windscreen damage, potholes, severe corrugations and cattle grids. There is little traffic on the roads but drivers must always be ready for the sudden appearance of roadtrains, which are large lorries pulling one or two long trailers that can literally blow other traffic off the road with the side draft, and produce clouds of dust and flying gravel. It is often best to slow or pull off the road until the roadtrain has passed. Other hazards include emus, kangaroos and stock which may suddenly run across the road. Many vehicles have 'roo-bars on the front which can save the engine from irreparable damage: this may mean the difference between driving away after an unavoidable impact and being left stranded in the remote outback. For those unfamiliar with driving in outback Australia it should be noted that one of the main causes of accidents is drivers falling asleep at the wheel. The roads are so long, straight and traffic free that it is hard to remain alert when travelling long distances. It is best to have frequent breaks, change drivers and maintain an interest in the countryside. The rule is to stop as soon as you begin to feel drowsy.

Service stations are generally infrequent away from the main roads and populated areas, so it is advisable to carry spare cans of fuel. Many areas are only accessible by four-wheel-drive vehicles with roads passing over sand ridges, creekbeds, rocks and salt lakes. Those travelling in remote areas should be able to cope with bogged vehicles and breakdowns, or travel in convoy. It is also advisable to be equipped with a radio to call for help if need arises and to inform others of travel plans before setting out. With daily temperatures of over 47°C common, especially in the north, all drivers should routinely carry plenty of drinking water in case of a breakdown.

## *TOWNS AND ACCOMMODATION*

The total population of Western Australia was 1.5 million in 1991 with 1.1 million of this concentrated in the Perth Metropolitan Area. Only a few other centres have substantial populations — notably Bunbury, Albany, Kalgoorlie, Geraldton and Port Hedland. The vast majority of the state is therefore virtually unpopulated. However accommodation is available in most small towns, especially on the south and west coasts, and also at all other major holiday destinations and mining centres. Many farms and pastoral stations also provide accommodation. Space precludes the inclusion here of the detailed information which can readily be obtained through tourist offices. Many of the older towns and buildings are full of surprises and charm.

## *NATIONAL PARKS AND RESERVES*

Western Australia has a comprehensive system of national parks, there being a total of 59 altogether. Many of the parks have facilities for camping and caravans. Up-to-date information can readily be obtained from park rangers or offices of the Department of Conservation and Land Management, or by writing to the head office at 50 Hayman Road, Como WA 6152. In the south-west the main parks include the Cape Arid, Cape Le Grand and Stokes Inlet National Parks near Esperance, and the Fitzgerald River, Stirling Range, Porongurup, Walpole-Nornalup and D'-Entrecasteaux National Parks near the south coast. There are many smaller parks along the west coast and in the hills near Perth. North of Perth are the popular Yanchep National Park and Nambung National Park, well known for the Pinnacles. Mt Lesueur near Jurien Bay, known for its extraordinarily diverse flora, is also destined to become a national park.

In the north-west the main parks include Kalbarri north of Geraldton, Cape Range near Exmouth, Karijini (Hamersley Range) and the Millstream-Chichester National Parks. Other large remote parks include the Collier Range south of Newman, and the Rudall River National Park in the Great Sandy Desert.

The Kimberley Region contains the large Drysdale River National Park and the scenic parks of Windjana Gorge, Tunnel Creek, Geikie Gorge, Hidden Valley, Purnululu (Bungle Bungle) and the Wolf Creek Meteorite Crater.

**A windmill typical of outback Western Australia. They are used to pump water for stock** *(BELOW)*
**Menzies Town Hall** *(BELOW RIGHT)*
**Falls on Garimbu Creek, north of the Prince Regent River**
*A.S. WESTON (OPPOSITE)*

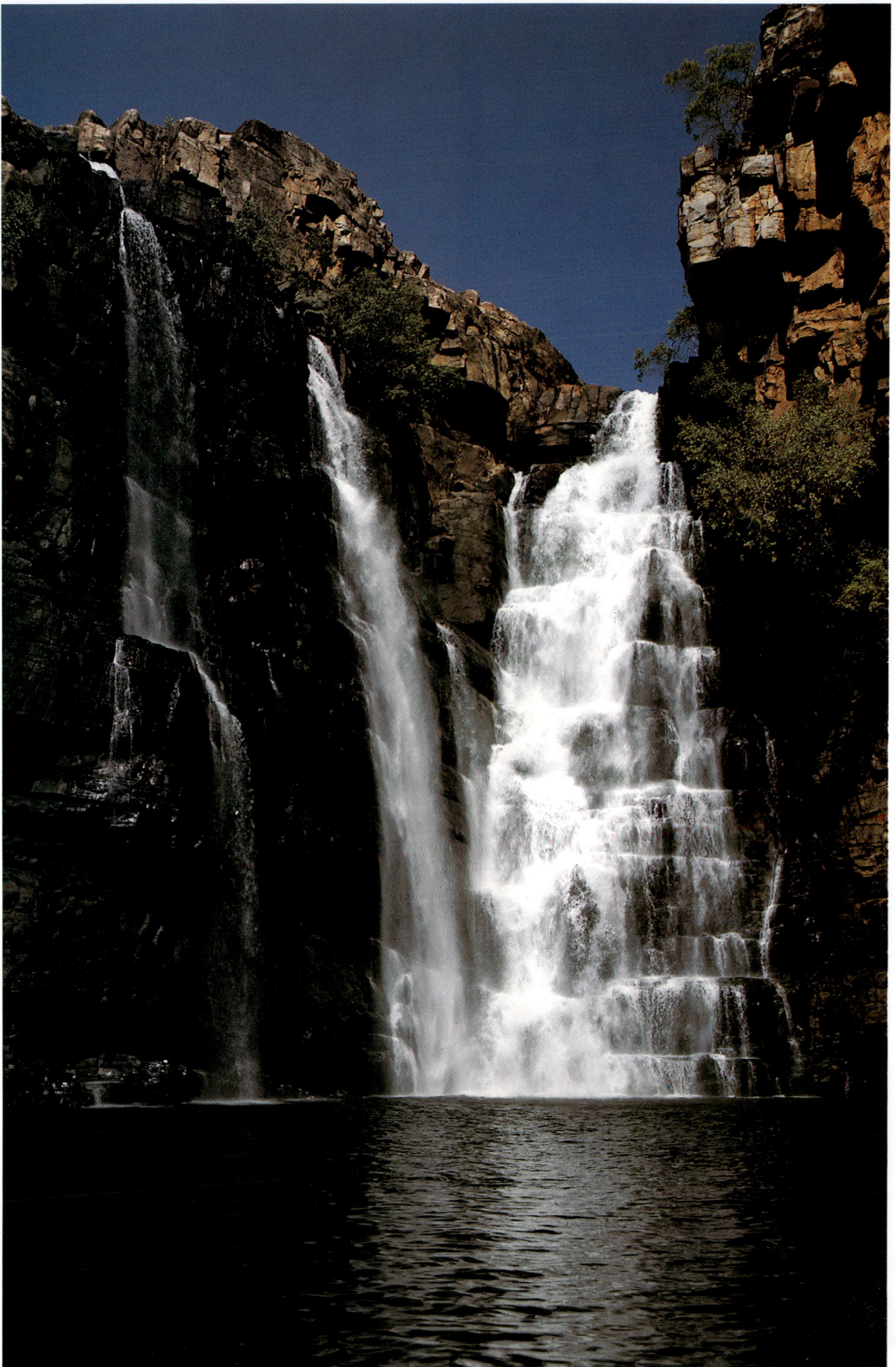

# *Vegetation*

THE WEST AUSTRALIAN vegetation varies greatly from one area to another, depending on such factors as rainfall, temperature extremes, topography, drainage and soil type, all of which are introduced in the previous sections of the book. In a brief summary of the vegetation it is best to break the country into three major regions: the South-west Province, the Eremaean Province, and the Northern Province. These are outlined in the vegetation map, which also indicates the distribution of the major types of vegetation. The map (frontispiece)is reproduced here by kind permission of Dr John Beard, from his book *Plant Life of Western Australia*. Description of the vegetation is completed by the inclusion of maritime plant associations and the vegetation of areas dominated by exotic species.

## The South-west Province

This Province extends up the west coast past Kalbarri to Shark Bay, and along the south coast to near Israelite Bay. Inland it extends to near Kalgoorlie, where it includes a transitional area between the Eremaean and South-west Provinces. It is the region with a Mediterranean-type climate of winter rainfall and hot dry summers. It is bounded by semi-arid land where the rainfall becomes too erratic for typical south-west vegetation. It has the greatest floral diversity, and inevitably in the section on the Flora, most examples come from this province. It may be appropriate to commence with the vegetation from the area with the highest rainfall, and progressively work towards the more arid parts of the region.

### *Karri Forest Region*

Near the south-west corner of the country this area receives rainfall from most approaching frontal systems. Its latitude and greater cloud cover also tend to reduce the amount of water loss, so that plants preferring more humid conditions thrive in this area.

The region is characterised by Karri trees (*Eucalyptus diversicolor*), which grow in places where there is a loamy soil, often on higher ground. These majestic trees grow to over 80 m tall (270 ft) and have a smooth, grey bark, which is shed once a year. The forest is found in a restricted area in the Pemberton-Walpole-Denmark region, and in isolated pockets near Augusta in the west, and on the Porongurup Range and Mt Manypeaks near Albany to the east.

**Karri Tree (***Eucalyptus diversicolor***)** *(LEFT)*
**Large Jarrah tree (***Eucalyptus marginata***) in the Jarrah forest with an undergrowth of Bull Banksia and Bracken** *(BELOW)*

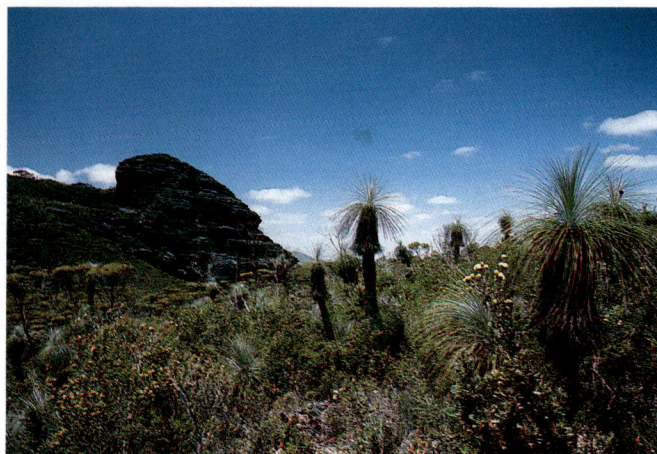

The understorey of the forest may be made up of Karri Hazel (*Trymalium floribundum*) which grows to about ten metres tall, Karri Oak (*Allocasuarina decussata*) and Peppermint (*Agonis flexuosa*). In the shrub layers there are a variety of plants such as Karri Hovea (*Hovea elliptica*), *Chorilaena quercifolia*, *Acacia pentadenia*, *Pimelia clavata*, *Hibbertia cuneiformis* and *Crowea angustifolia*. Herbs and creepers include *Clematis pubescens*, *Hardenbergia comptoniana*, *Anigozanthos flavidus*, *Orthrosanthus laxus* and orchids such as the Slipper Orchid (*Cryptostylis ovata*).

Areas of sand, gravel and rock may have mainly species typical of Jarrah forest, with some large Marri trees (*Eucalyptus calophylla*), or Bullich (*E. megacarpa*), which has a blue-grey bark. Near the south coast at Walpole there is an area with a particularly high summer rainfall where the Karri forest includes huge Red Tingle trees (*E. jacksonii*). Poorly drained areas near rivers and streams have Flooded Gums (*Eucalyptus rudis*), River Banksia (*B. seminuda*), Karri Cedar (*Agonis juniperina*) and Native Willow (*Oxylobium lanceolatum*). Coastal areas have extensive tracts of swamp with a wide variety of shrubs and herbs, especially paperbarks (*Melaleuca* spp.), bottlebrushes such as *Beaufortia sparsa*, kinds of boronia, triggerplants (*Stylidium*), sundews (*Drosera*), and the Albany Pitcher Plant (*Cephalotus follicularis*). Sandhills may be covered in Peppermint trees (*Agonis flexuosa*), or between Walpole and Denmark the Red Flowering Gum (*Eucalyptus ficifolia*) may be found.

## The Jarrah Forest

This is characterised by the Jarrah tree (*Eucalyptus marginata*), which grows best on laterite found in the Darling Range, stretching from north of Perth to the south coast. The tree will grow on a variety of soils, including coastal sand, and extends well beyond the Jarrah forest area, sometimes having a mallee growth-form in low rainfall areas.

The Jarrah forest usually has Jarrah as the dominant tree mixed with Marri (*E. calophylla*) and, less commonly, Blackbutt (*E. patens*). Understorey trees include Bull Banksia (*B. grandis*), Snottygobble (*Persoonia elliptica*) and *Allocasuarina fraseriana*. Under the trees there is an enormously complex shrub and herb vegetation made up of a large number of species, many of which are illustrated in the Flora section, such as *Hakea lissocarpha*, *Dryandra sessilis*, *Grevillea wilsonii*, *Tetratheca nuda*, *Hibbertia hypericoides*, *Bossiaea aquifolium*, Zamia Palms, grass trees and many sundews and orchids.

## South Coastal Vegetation

The climate becomes progressively less humid east of Albany and the vegetation takes on heath-like characteristics in well-drained areas. These have a very diverse flora, with many woody shrubs including *Banksia nutans*, *B. sphaerocarpa*, *B. coccinea*, species of *Dryandra*, Chittick (*Lambertia inermis*) and many varieties of bottlebrush, including kinds of *Calothamnus*, *Melaleuca*, and *Beaufor-*

**Heath with Tallerack (*Eucalyptus tetragona*) near the Stirling Range. This mallee is characteristic of the area — it is often grown in gardens for its attractive foliage** *(LEFT)*
**Montane vegetation on the Stirling Range with grass trees (*Kingia*), small mallees (*Eucalyptus redunca*) and flowering Mountain Kunzea (*K. recurva*) and *Darwinia* (red)** *(ABOVE)*

*tia*. The glaucous leaves of the mallee Tallerack (*Eucalyptus tetragona*) are characteristic of these heathlands. In low lying areas there may be dense mallee woodland, or thickets of *Banksia speciosa*.

## South Coastal Ranges

The Stirling Range and the Barrens in the Fitzgerald River National Park have heath-like vegetation made up of large numbers of plants which are entirely restricted to the mountains. The Stirling Range is best known for the variety of mountain bells (*Darwinia*). There are also Mountain Peas (*Nemcia icaceana*), unique species of *Banksia*, such as *B. brownii* and *B. solandri*, Giant Andersonia (*A. axilliflora*), and *Isopogon latifolius*.

The Barrens are also a botanist's paradise with shrubs like Royal Hakea (*H. victoriae*), Barrens Regelia (*R. velutina*), Qualup Bell (*Pimelia physodes*), and the Crown-fruited Mallee (*Eucalyptus coronata*).

The south coastal granite hills also have some interesting vegetation such as the Karri forest on the Porongurup Range, which has unique species of *Villarsia*. The hills at Mt Le Grand and Mt Arid east of Esperance have some unusual species like the Coastal Hakea (*H. clavata*), which has thick succulent leaves, and the very attractive bottlebrush, *Kunzea baxteri*.

## Wheatbelt

The wide variety of soil types and drainage patterns lead to there being many differing vegetations found in the area. On the eastern side of the Darling Range there is an area of Wandoo woodland (*Eucalyptus wandoo*), which has an attractive grey-white bark. Further east this gives way to Powder-Bark Wandoo (*E. accedens*) on gravelly hills, which has a warmer, pinkish bark. York Gum (*E. loxophleba*) becomes more common in this area. It has a dark, persistent bark, especially on the trunk. In the south Flat-topped Yates (*E. occidentalis*) are common in low-lying areas, while the Salmon Gum (*E. salmonophloia*) is found all through the Wheatbelt. It grows in heavy clay soils which were considered best for farming, and so little of the original cover remains — in fact most of the Wheatbelt vegetation has now been cleared for agriculture. Remaining areas are mostly heathland of little economic value. Fortunately these areas have some of the richest vegetations and in spring produce attractive displays of wildflowers, including featherflowers (*Verticordia*), and species of *Grevillea*, especially *G.*

*eriostachya* and *G. petrophiloides.*

Extensive areas of swamp and saltlake are found in the Wheatbelt. Before farming many would have been freshwater, but farming increased run-off and salination killing most of the natural vegetation and only leaving salt-tolerant species, such as the Sheoak (*Casuarina obesa*), Salt Paperbark (*Melaleuca cuticularis*) and a herb layer of samphires and other Chenopodiaceae.

## West Coastal Sandplains and Hills

This area stretches from Perth to Shark Bay and includes a variety of vegetations. Banksia woodland is very important, with the main species being *B. menziesii, B. attenuata,* and *B. prionotes.* The complexity appears to increase northwards to Jurien Bay and Eneabba where there is a very rich heathland vegetation growing on laterite and sandplain. The small, bushy tree *Eucalyptus todiana is* common, and patches of Wandoo (*E. wandoo*). The Illyarrie (*E. erythrocorys*) with large, yellow flowers also grows in this area. Woody Pear (*Xylomelum angustifolium*) is present, also many kinds of *Dryandra* and the Black Kangaroo Paw (*Macropidia fuliginosa*). Many Wheatbelt and desert species approach the coast further north where the climate becomes more arid, including the tall, spindly Desert Poplar (*Codonocarpus cotinifolius* — Gyrostemonaceae).

**Heath vegetation, known locally as kwongan, characteristic of many areas in the south-west. This is in the Wheatbelt area near Lake Grace with species of featherflower (*Verticordia*), and shrubs including a sheoak** (BELOW)

**Hampton Tableland on the edge of the Nullarbor Plain. Bluebush (*Maireana sedifolia*) is the dominant plant. The small tree Western Myall (*Acacia papyrocarpa*) is common on the edges of the plain** (BOTTOM)

**Powder-bark Wandoo (*Eucalyptus accedens*) usually has a shrub cover including Box Poison (*Gastrolobium parviflorum*)** (RIGHT)

**Vegetation on the Barrens Ranges in the Fitzgerald River National Park. The Barrens Regelia (*R. velutina*) is prominent on the quartzite rocks** (OPPOSITE)

# The Eremaean Province

This forms seventy per cent of the land area of Western Australia and is characterised by low and unreliable rainfall. It is technically all desert, but unlike most perceptions of 'desert' the area is almost entirely vegetated. This is partly because the Australian desert is very ancient compared to some other desert regions of the world, and plant life has had time to adapt to the conditions. It may also be partly due to there having been no pastoral activity in Australia until European settlement — many deserts have been created or extended by indigenous peoples overgrazing the land with their domestic animals. The arid region of Australia was much more extensive during the last ice age, 17,000 years ago, when the climate was much more severe. The plant life is probably now enjoying relatively benign conditions compared to those under which it evolved.

## The Nullarbor Region

This is a flat, limestone plain devoid of trees. The area extends into South Australia and has a low vegetation primarily of Blue Bush (*Maireana sedifolia*), which is adapted to saline and alkaline soils, and grasses such as *Stipa eremophila*. Near the edges of the plain there are small trees, especially Western Myall (*Acacia papyrocarpa*). Near the coast various gum trees grow as mallees, especially *Eucalyptus socialis*. 'Mallee' is a growth-form where the trees have many slim stems usually growing from a basal rootstock or lignotuber. Areas of mallee are fire prone, and the trees usually regenerate from the rootstock, although some are killed by the fire and regenerate as dense, even-aged stands from seed germinating after fires.

## Mulga Woodland

This comprises a large central area which has little rain, tending to fall more during the winter months. It is a scrub or woodland mainly with a variety of wattles, especially Mulga (*Acacia aneura*), Bowgada (*A. linophylla*) and Kurara (*A. tetragonophylla*). Other shrubs include Sandalwood (*Santalum spicatum*), species of *Cassia* and poverty bushes (*Eremophila*). Clay soils near water courses and saltlakes often have extensive areas of everlasting daisies in July-August. These may become very widespread when seeds build up after a series of good years.

## Spinifex Steppe

This vegetation covers a large part of Western Australia. It occurs in semi-arid and arid areas mainly where rainfall is more likely to occur in summer, or where it is very unreliable. Scattered trees are found over most of the area, such as Snappy Gums, now known as Mygum, (*Eucalyptus leucophloia*) in the Pilbara region, and wattles, including Rangi Bush (*Acacia pyrifolia*). Ground vegetation often includes extensive areas of mulla mulla (*Ptilotus*). The spinifex grasslands were managed by Aborigines, who burned large areas each year. Fire favours spinifex, much of which would be replaced by mulga in the absence of fire, and patches of mulga often reflect a past tradition of protecting certain areas from fire. Since Aboriginal management ceased, wildfires have become more extensive and uncontrolled. They are often started by lightning strikes and burn the once-protected areas of mulga. These fires may burn for months on end, sweeping through large parts of the Kimberley and Pilbara regions. Attempts are now being made to try and reinstate Aboriginal fire management to restore the vegetation and conserve the flora and natural wildlife.

## Rivers and Billabongs

When rain comes in arid regions, it is often heavy and the resulting run-off fills dry watercourses and produces large areas of temporary swamp. The increased water availability in these areas produces an attractive vegetation characterised by River Gums (*Eucalyptus camaldulensis*) and Coolabahs (*E. microtheca*). Other gum trees include the small-leaved *E. aspera* and Bloodwood (*E. patellaris*). The Ghost Gum (*E. papuana*) is found in the more arid regions near Warburton and in the eastern Kimberley. The Cajeput tree (*Melaleuca leucadendra*) is common along rivers in the Pilbara, especially Millstream and the Hamersley Gorges. The fan palm, *Livistona alfredii*, is also found at Millstream. The stony bases of dry creeks and areas of plain where rainwater collects often have a thick growth of Sturt Peas (*Clianthus formosus*).

## Ranges

Cape Range, near Exmouth, has in interesting vegetation including some species which are common in the Kimberley Region, such as the Flame Tree or Yulbah (*Erythrina vespertilio*), and Rock

Morning Glory (*Ipomoea costata*). There are also many Rock Figs (*Ficus platypoda*), a species found in rocky areas across northern Australia. It is an important food resource for the Bowerbird.

# The Northern Province

This area is influenced by a summer monsoonal rainfall, which is relatively reliable, with the wet season extending up to six months in the northern part. The vegetation mainly consists of hot-tropical savannah and scrublands.

## Western Kimberley

This area has a relatively dry climate with only a short summer wet season. It has a savannah grassland, often of blue grass and ribbon grass, or species of spinifex. There are large areas where the main trees are Pindan (*Acacia eriopoda*), which unlike mulga is encouraged by fires as long as they are not too frequent. In other areas the trees include Woollybutt (*Eucalyptus miniata*), Baobabs (*Adansonia gregorii*) and Coolabahs (*Eucalyptus microtheca*).

## Eastern Kimberley

This area is semi-arid with only a short summer wet period. The vegetation is mainly made up of various grasses, with spinifex on the hilly areas and other short grasses on the plains and clay areas. Stunted trees may include the Snappy Gum (*Eucalyptus brevifolia*), and species of *Terminalia* (Combretaceae). Shrubs include kinds of *Grevillea*, *Acacia* and *Hakea*. Some of the vegetation is very similar to that in the Pilbara Region.

## Central Kimberley

This is a dry tropical area with a four month summer wet season. The main vegetation is made up of grasses such as Curly Spinifex (*Plectrachne pungens*) and ribbon grass mixed with low trees such as Snappy Gum (*Eucalyptus brevifolia*) and other gums including *E. dichromophloia* and *E. perfoliata*. Baobabs are also present. Shrubs include species of *Hibiscus*, the yellow-flowered Kapok Tree (*Cochlospermum fraseri*) and kinds of wild fig (*Ficus*).

## Northern Kimberley

This is a hot dry tropical area with a four to six month summer wet season bringing over 700 mm rainfall. The vegetation is made up of woodland with a tall grass groundcover. The trees include

**Mulga woodland near Payne's Find. This mainly comprises various species of wattle with very little plant growth underneath, apart from annual herbs after winter rain, especially everlasting daisies** (LEFT)
**Spinifex steppe on sand ridges. This vegetation is typical of a large part of the Eremaean Province. This patch has escaped a recent fire and has flowering *Plechtrachne* and *Triodia* hummock grasses** (BELOW)

Messmate (*Eucalyptus tetradonta*) and Woollybutt (*E. miniata*), which has attractive orange flowers. Screwpines (*Pandanus*) and fan palms (*Livistona*) are common, together with many tropical trees such as *Terminalia* sp. (Combretaceae) and kinds of desert walnut (*Owenia* spp.). Underneath there is usually a tall growth of grass, especially *Sorghum*, which may grow to up to two metres high. Open areas in the southern part may have extensive growths of the mulla mulla *Gomphrena canescens*.

Much interest has been centered recently on the presence in the area of vine thickets which bear resemblance to tropical rainforest vegetation. These thickets are common in north Queensland but were not thought to be in Western Australia until they were found in 1961. They are fire resistant and contain a variety of tropical trees and shrubs bound together by vines, which make them almost impenetrable.

## Maritime Vegetation

The marine environment and coastal dunes have distinct vegetations. Below low tide marks around the West Australian coast there are extensive areas of sea grasses, which mainly grow on sandy areas. These plants are more allied to pondweeds than grass and provide food and habitat for many marine animals. They are the main food source of the Dugong, which lives in the Shark Bay area. Mangrove vegetation is common along shores in the north with many kinds of mangrove tree. Mangroves grow in estuarine areas and on mudflats. A small isolated area of mangrove is found in the Leschenault Inlet near Bunbury.

Dune vegetation usually has a growth of Coastal Spinifex (*S. hirsutus* and *S. longifolius*), Sword Sedge (*Lepidosperma*), Dune Scaevola (*S. crassifolia*), Pigface (*Carpobrotus virescens*) and the grey Coastal Daisybush (*Olearia axillaris*). In the north, Beach Morning Glory (*Ipomoea pes-caprae*) is common. Behind the fore-dune in the southern part of the area, several wattles are common, especially groves of *Acacia rostellifera*, scattered *A. cyclops*, and the thorny-leaved *A. littorea*.

## Unnatural Vegetation

Since European settlement began the natural bushland has been systematically replaced by plants from other parts of the world. Much of the south-west is now covered by an annual growth of wheat and introduced fodder plants, especially European grasses and subterranean clover, while many forest areas have been replaced by exotic pine trees, especially *Pinus radiata*. Early set-

tlers, as well as bringing in crop species, also brought wild and garden plants from England, because they were nostalgic about their homeland. Many plants have also arrived by accident in hay and other materials transported to Australia.

Most of the vegetation in the farmed areas of the country is now almost entirely made up of exotic plants; this is because native species are not adapted to farming, and to growing in soil with added fertilizers. Native species are also quickly replaced by exotic weeds in bushland areas where fertilizer has been added. Remaining trees survive for some years but eventually die from ringbarking by stock, or by excessive insect attack following increased fertilizer use and loss of natural predators. Stock grazing prevents any regeneration. Fortunately farmers have seen the need for trees and are now replanting them in fenced enclosures, especially in areas where salt has become a problem.

Spring flowers in farmed land are often spectacular: plants include the daisy Capeweed (*Arctotheca calendula*), Paterson's Curse (*Echium plantagineum*), Cape Tulip (*Homeria miniata*), and Soursob (*Oxalis pes-caprae*). Many garden plants introduced from South Africa are adapted to similar conditions in their native country and are spreading into bushland areas. They include gladioli, freesias, baboon flowers, watsonias and afternoon flowers (*Hesperantha*). The South African veldt grass is also an aggressive colonizer of some areas. Swampy areas are often colonized by calla lilies (*Araceae*) and in some places by canna lilies and Taro (*Colocasia esculenta*).

Doublegee (*Emex australis*) from South Africa is a painful weed for barefoot travellers, while Mesquite forms thorny bushes in the north together with *Acacia farnesiana*, which was probably brought to Australia from Central America by the Portuguese before Captain Cook. Attempts are being made to eradicate Mesquite, while outbreaks of Skeleton Weed (*Chondrilla juncea* — a daisy) have so far been successfully destroyed.

Coastal dunes have introduced plants which help stabilize the sand, such as the South African Pigface, Marram Grass, Evening Primrose, Onion Weed, and Sea Kale. As well as plants from other parts of the world, some species native to other parts of Australia are becoming aggressive colonizers in bushland areas, such as a kurrajong from New South Wales and Black Wattle.

Other factors which are modifying the natural vegetation include the changes in fire frequency and intensity since Aboriginal management was replaced by European management. This has had indirect effects, including changes in grazing by native animals, which may prevent regeneration of some plants. Introduced grazing species also have a marked influence on regenerating vegetation, especially rabbits, sheep and cattle. On the other hand it must be remembered that in the early days of Aboriginal management the vegetation was very much influenced by massive grazing mammals such as diprotodons and giant kangaroos which are now extinct — perhaps our large grazing species have

**Coastal vegetation on Rottnest Island with Spinifex grass**
(*S. longifolius*), **Sword Sedge, green** *Scaevola crassifolia*, **and grey**
**Coastal Daisybush** (*BELOW*)
**Capeweed and Sheep's Sorrel** (*RIGHT*)

**Agriculture has changed the soil by increasing runoff and salination. This kills the native vegetation, and it is eventually replaced by salt-tolerant species**

reinstated some elements of these earlier grazing and browsing patterns.

Air pollution, especially near cities, is also adding unnatural levels of nitrates, sulphates, carbon dioxide and other fertilizers which affect the growth of plants. These changes encourage some insect populations, which in turn influence survival of individual plants, all of which results in long-term change in the vegetation.

# *FLORA*

Western Australia covers an enormous area stretching from temperate to tropical climates, and from rainforest to arid conditions. As might be expected from such a range of conditions the flora is very diverse, containing a vast array of species which have evolved in the area since Australia was part of the great southern continent, Gondwanaland. At that time it shared its flora and fauna with Africa and South America; that is why so many Australian plant families are also found in these countries, the most notable example being the Proteaceae, which is also well represented in South Africa. Another element of the flora mainly has common origins with that of south-east Asia, many plants having crossed into Australia as the land mass moved northwards. The remaining flora, which comprises the majority of the vegetation in farmland and settled areas, has been brought here by accident or design since European settlement.

The south-west is acknowledged as having one of the most diverse floras in the world, having many similarities with the Cape region of South Africa. The great variety of plants seems to have been the result of long-term isolation and factors such as severe drought during ice ages and sea level changes. Together these factors have resulted in the fragmentation of plant populations into small patches, which have remained isolated long enough for them to evolve into new species.

It is impossible to do the flora justice in this small volume; however, examples are illustrated from most families and important genera to serve as an introduction to the region. Grasses and sedges deserve more specialist treatment, and so are not covered in detail; similarly some of the lesser known families are omitted. Other families familiar to gardeners and visitors to the country are also not included, mainly because the plants are inconspicuous or have very few Australian species. These include the Pink family, Caryophyllaceae (8 spp.), Cabbage family, Cruciferae (41 spp.), Stonecrop family, Crassulaceae (8 spp.), Saxifrage family, Saxifragaceae (1 sp.), Rose family, Rosaceae (4 spp.), Primrose family, Primulaceae (3 spp.), Bedstraw family, Rubiaceae (41 spp.), and the Cucumber family, Cucurbitaceae (7 spp.).

The plants are arranged in an order used by botanists (Cronquist, 1981) so that the text is easier to use in conjunction with other books (e.g. *Flora of the Perth Region*, 1987).

## Ferns and Allied Forms

Although generally associated with cool damp conditions, there are some ferns adapted to living in hot arid areas. However, most species are found growing in damp shady conditions. The group includes two minute club-mosses and two species of *Selaginella*. There are nine kinds of quillwort (*Isoetes*), which are small plants often found growing on the bottom of pools on the top of granite domes. Water ferns include the very attractive nardoo ferns (*Mar-silea*), which have floating leaves arranged in the form of a cross. They often grow in arid areas where water collects after rain, and have nut-like sporocarps which are resistant to drought. There are also two species of *Azolla*, which look like lichens floating on water. The introduced *Salvinia* is another fern — it is popular with aquarium keepers and has become a serious weed problem in some places. Beetles are being used to control it in Queensland. The Indian Water Fern (*Ceratopteris thalictroides*) chokes fast-flowing spring waters at Millstream in the Pilbara. Bracken is common in the south-west especially in the Karri forest area. There are six kinds of bracken in the world; the Australian species is *Pteridium esculentum*.

### *Adiantum*
Maidenhair ferns are familiar to most people with their soft rounded leaflets and delicate growth form, much used by florists. There are four species in the area.

**A. aethiopicum** occurs in wetter areas from Perth to Albany, especially on damp clay banks or among rocks in shady forests.

**Venus Hair Fern, A. capillus-veneris,** grows in gorges in the Hamersley Range.

### *Cheilanthes*
These are probably the most commonly seen ferns, generally growing on rocks. There are about 180 species in the genus altogether with eight occurring in the west.

**Rock Fern, C. austrotenuifolia,** is widespread in the south-west and extends across the southern part of Australia and into New Zealand.

**Mulga Fern, C. sieberi,** occurs in rock crevices and extends into the arid interior from the Kimberley to the south coast.

### *Ophioglossum*
Unusual small ferns; about 55 species are known with two in Western Australia.

**Austral Adder's Tongue, O. lusitanicum,** occurs from Exmouth to Kalgoorlie.

## Cycads — Cycadopsida

### *Macrozamia*
Cycads are very palm-like in appearance and include the Sago Palm. In Australia there are 14 species with only one member of the genus in Western Australia, although the related *Cycas lanepoolei* occurs in the Kimberley.

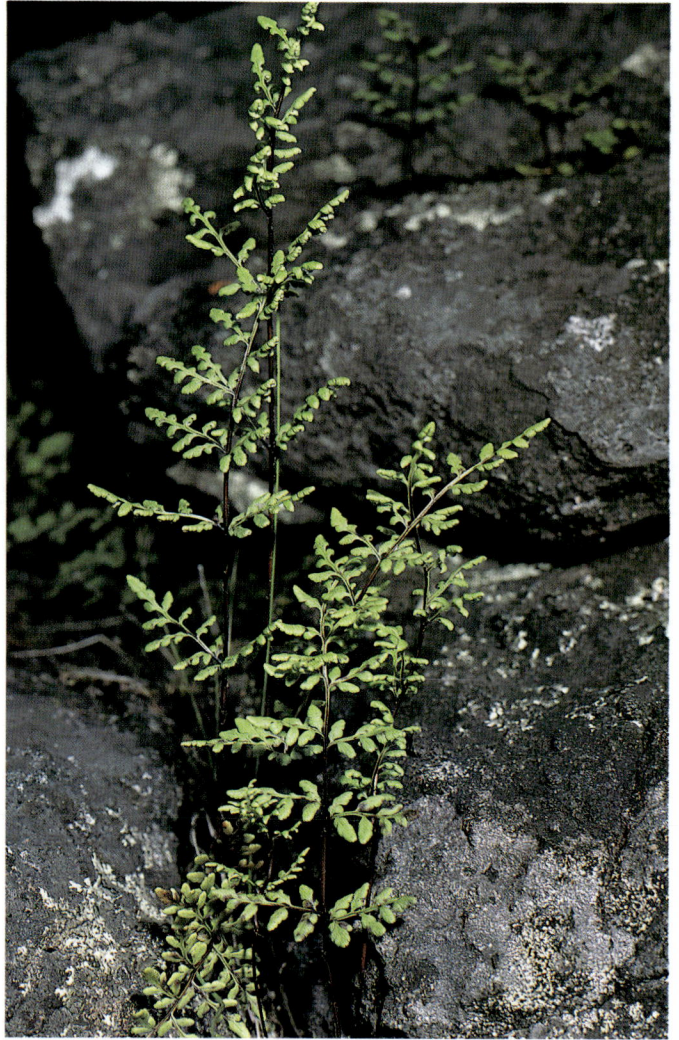

*Selaginella gracillima* (LEFT)
*Cheilanthes austrotenuifolia* (ABOVE)

**Zamia Palm, *M. riedlei*,** is widespread between Eneabba and Esperance. It varies in growth form from having virtually no trunk to plants having a trunk up to two metres high — especially near Esperance. The palms have cones, which are either male or female. The female cones produce large orange-coated seeds, which are poisonous unless treated. They formed an important food source for the local Aborigines.

## Conifers — Coniferopsida

The conifers include the introduced Radiata Pine, which is extensively grown in forestry plantations. The native species include the Wild Plum, *Podocarpus drouynianus* which is a many-stemmed bush that grows mainly in the south-west corner from Augusta to Albany. The cypress family, Cupressaceae, includes three species of *Actinostrobus*, which are densely branched shrubs occurring in sandy soils subject to inundation in the south-west, and five species of *Callitris*.

**Rottnest Island Pine, *Callitris preissii*,** grows up to six metres tall and is widespread in the south-west and extends as far as Victoria.

***C. glaucophylla*** is widespread in the Eremaean Province growing on sand and in rocky areas. It grows on the rocky slopes of the Hamersley Range gorges where it can escape fires burning through the spinifex.

## Palms — Arecaceae

(As monocotyledons palms are botanically distant from cycads and conifers, but are included here because they have superficial similarities.) Attractive fan palms occur near water in the Kimberley and Pilbara regions.

**Millstream Fan Palm, *Livistona alfredii*,** is a feature of Millstream National Park where it has been isolated from similar palms for so long that it has become a distinct species. Date palms and California fan palms are also found growing at Millstream. *L. eastonii* and *L. loriphylla* grow in the Kimberley.

**Screw pines, *Pandanus***
These are more closely allied to reeds than palms or pines. They occur mainly in coastal areas in tropical regions of the world. Several species are found in the northern Kimberley.

## The Laurel Family — Lauraceae

This is a large family of evergreen trees and shrubs containing over 2000 species in the world. Most are found in the tropics, but laurel is a common tree in England.

***Cassytha***
The Laurel family is only represented here by the dodder laurels.

*Livistona alfredii* (TOP LEFT)
*Cassytha* (TOP RIGHT)
*Clematis pubescens* (Jul.-Oct.) (BOTTOM RIGHT)
*Ranunculus colonorum* (Sep.-Dec.) (ABOVE)

These are parasitic plants similar to dodder, forming dense tangled mats over trees and shrubs. There are ten species and the genus extends into Africa, Indonesia, New Guinea and New Zealand. (True dodder, *Cuscuta*, belongs to an unrelated family, allied to *Convolvulus*. (It is a more delicate, reddish-coloured plant which originates from Europe, but is now found in most parts of the world, including south-west Australia).

## The Buttercup Family — Ranunculaceae

This family contains over two thousand species, mainly in northern temperate parts of the world. The family includes many cultivated varieties, especially species of *Anemone*, *Aquilegia* and *Clematis*.

### *Clematis*

These are attractive climbing plants producing masses of white flowers in early spring, and white, feathery clusters of seeds. Three species are found in the south-west.

**Old Man's Beard, *C. microphylla,*** extends from Kalbarri to Israelite Bay, growing mainly on coastal limestone and sands.

*C. pubescens* occurs further inland, on the Darling Scarp and in the Karri Forest.

## *Ranunculus*

About 400 species of buttercup are known, seven of them from Western Australia. They are mainly found growing in damp places in the south-west.

**Buttercup, *R. colonorum,*** is an attractive herb with bright yellow flowers and grows up to about 0.5 m tall. *Hibbertia hypericoides* is also locally known as a buttercup because of its yellow flowers, although belonging to an unrelated family, Dilleniaceae.

## The Sheoak Family — Casuarinaceae

The sheoaks are mainly shrubs or trees with fine green branchlets — they are not leaves in the true sense (the leaves are reduced to rings of minute scales, which encircle the branchlets). The wood has a very oak-like grain, but otherwise they have little in common with oak trees. The female trees have cone-like fruits containing winged seeds and the males long catkins. There are about 80 species altogether, mainly occurring in Australia with some extending to Burma and Fiji.

### *Allocasuarina*

Most Australian sheoaks belong to this genus, which has its scale-like leaves in whorls of 4-10 as opposed to 12-15 in *Casuarina*.

*A. fraseriana* is the most frequently seen sheoak away from water from Jurien Bay to near Albany.

*A. huegeliana* grows mainly on granite outcrops in the south-west.

*A. humilis* is a common shrub species.

**Compass Tree, *A. pinaster,*** is an interesting pine-like shrub growing on sandplain areas near Lake Grace. The name comes from its habit of leaning to the south.

### *Casuarina*

This genus has scale leaves in whorls of 12-15. Only two species occur in Western Australia.

**Swamp Sheoak, *C. obesa,*** is a tree up to 10 m tall which grows along riversides and swamps, mainly in saline conditions. It occurs from Kalbarri to Israelite Bay and inland to Kalgoorlie. It is also found across southern Australia to New South Wales.

## The Iceplant Family — Aizoaceae

The family is well-known to gardeners from the brilliant daisy-like flowers of *Mesembrianthemum*. The family includes over 2500 species worldwide, with many in South Africa and Australia. Some genera, such as *Tetragonia* (bower spinach), have little resemblance to daisies; these are green herbs with minute yellow flowers, which grow on coastal sand-dunes.

### *Carpobrotus*

Large creeping succulent plants which grow on sand dunes and around salt lakes. They have daisy-like flowers.

**Pigface, *C. virescens,*** has beautiful pink flowers up to 6 cm across. *C. edulis* is more commonly found; it has yellow and pink flowers, and comes from South Africa.

*Disphyma crassifolium* has smaller flowers and cylindrical leaves. It is widely distributed in inland areas, especially around salt lakes. It used to be included in the genus *Carpobrotus*.

## The Spinach Family — Chenopodiaceae

This cosmopolitan family contains about 1500 species of herbs and shrubs with small green flowers. Mostly they are adapted to living in arid regions and in saline environments. The family is well represented in Australia, with some species forming important forage plants in arid areas, especially blue bush, *Maireana* (formerly known as *Kochia*), which are widespread, especially on the Nullarbor Plain. The family includes the samphires, *Halosarcia* and *Sarcocornia*, which are fleshy succulents found in salt marshes and salt lakes.

**Berry Saltbush, *Rhagodia baccata,*** grows into a spreading leafy shrub and produces large numbers of red berries which attract small birds, especially white-eyes (silvereyes).

*Disphyma crassifolia* (Aug.-Nov.) *(LEFT)*
*Ptilotus manglesii* (Sep.-Jan.) *(BELOW)*

*Calandrinia liniflora* (Sep.-Nov.) *(LEFT)*
*Hibbertia hypericoides* (Apr.-Nov.) *(ABOVE)*

**Prickly Saltwort, *Salsola kali,*** is widespread all over Australia and is also found in Europe and Asia. The dried-up plants become tumbleweeds, rolling great distances across flat areas. It is possibly not native to Australia. (The tumbleweed of North America is *Amaranthus albus* and belongs to the next family.)

# The Amaranth Family — Amaranthaceae

This family contains a number of cultivated garden plants, especially species of *Amaranthus*, *Celosia* and *Iresine*. There are about 900 species, which are mainly found in tropical and subtropical regions of the world.

## *Ptilotus*

This is the best-known genus in Australia, containing the attractive mulla mullas, which are so characteristic of the north and inland areas. About 80 species are known from Western Australia.

**Rose-tipped Mulla Mulla, *P. manglesii,*** is common in the Darling Range near Perth.

**Hairy Mulla Mulla, *P. helipteroides,*** and Tall Mulla Mulla, *P. exaltatus*, carpet large areas of the Pilbara region in late winter.

# The Purslane Family — Portulacaceae

A small family of about 500 species and 20 genera. The plants are mainly small annual or perennial herbs and are often succulent. *Portulaca grandiflora* from Argentina is often grown in gardens.

## *Calandrinia*

These are mainly succulent annuals which grow on exposed bare ground using water stored in leaves and stems to continue growing after the soil dries out. The flowers are often a vibrant, glowing pink.

**Parakeelya, *C. polyandra,*** is widespread from the north-west coast to the Nullarbor and is also present in the Kimberley.

***C. liniflora*** is common nearer the coast from Kalbarri to near Augusta.

# The Hibbertia Family — Dilleniaceae

Plants in this family range from trees to herbs and include some climbing species. The family has about 350 species, which mainly grow in tropical and sub-tropical regions. The vine *Hibbertia scan-*

*dens* is native to Queensland and widely grown in gardens.

## *Hibbertia*

These plants are usually yellow-flowered shrubs although some have orange flowers. There are about 68 species in Western Australia, with most occurring in the south-west. One is found in the Pilbara and two in the Kimberley region.

**Buttercup, *H. hypericoides,*** is a very common species found from near Geraldton in the north to Augusta. Some plants can be found flowering during most months of the year.

**Orange Stars, *H. stellaris,*** has orange flowers in the southern part of its range; further north near Perth it has yellow flowers. It grows in wet areas around swamps.

**Cutleaf Hibbertia, *H. cuneiformis,*** is the tall species common in the Karri forest.

**Large Hibbertia, *H. lasiopus,*** is a large-flowered, low shrub in the Jarrah forest.

# The Kurrajong Family — Sterculiaceae

Most of these plants are shrubs or trees found in tropical and subtropical regions, although many are also found in more temperate areas in South Africa and Australia. About 1200 species are known. The flowers of *Thomasia* are interesting because they have a similar appearance to those of the tomato family, Solanaceae.

## *Brachychiton*

This genus includes the kurrajong trees and the Illawarra Flame Tree native to Queensland and New South Wales. Kurrajongs occur mainly in the Pilbara and Kimberley districts, where 8 species are known, although a species from New South Wales has become naturalized in Kings Park.

**Kurrajong** (formerly ***B. australe***) has bright green lobed leaves and grows in the Pilbara district.

## *Lasiopetalum*

This is a genus endemic to Australia. It includes about 24 species in the west.

***L. floribundum*** is a densely branched shrub which has

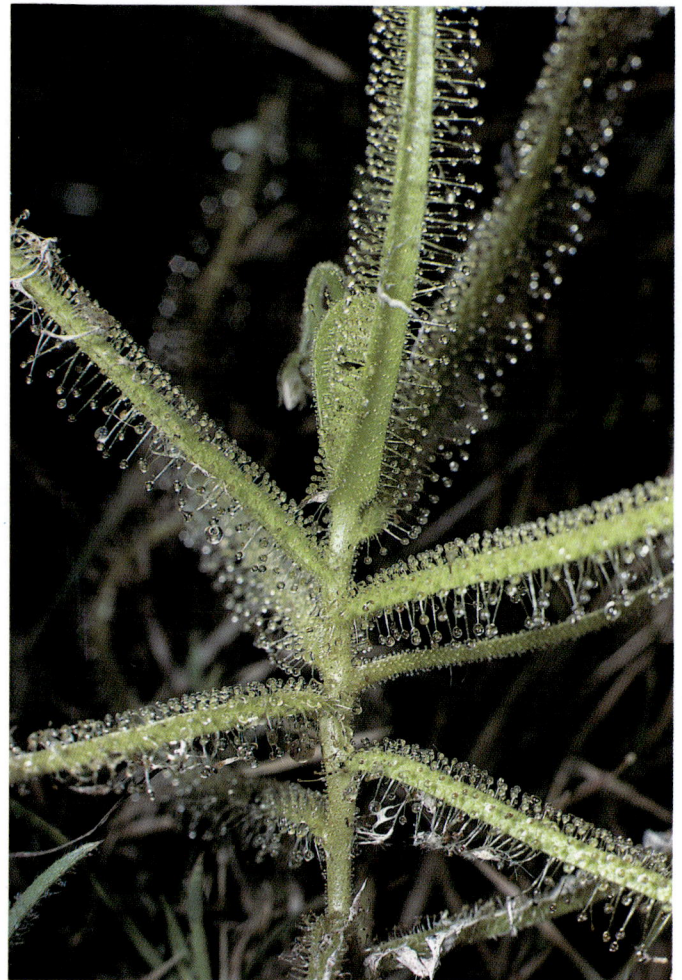

*Alyogyne huegelii* (Sep.-Dec.) *(TOP LEFT)*
*Drosera indica* (May-Aug.) *(RIGHT)*
*Drosera menziesii* (Aug.-Nov.) *(ABOVE)*

masses of flowers in spring. It is found mainly in the Jarrah forest.

## The Baobab Family — Bombacaceae

Sometimes put in the Hibiscus family these trees are found from Australia to Africa. They have swollen, bottle-like trunks which store water.

### *Adansonia*

Only one species is present in the Kimberley district.

**Baobab, *A. gregorii*,** also grows at Cossack in the Pilbara, where the tree was probably planted.

## The Hibiscus Family — Malvaceae

The family includes many garden plants, especially hibiscus and mallow, and also economic species such as cotton. There are about 1500 species in tropical and temperate regions of the world. Kinds of wild cotton, *Gossypium*, grow naturally in the north-west and Kimberley regions.

In the south the main representatives of the family are species of wild hibiscus. Some classifications put most species in the Baobab family, Bombacaceae.

**Wild Hibiscus, *Alyogyne huegelii*,** normally has an attractive mauve flower, but a yellow-flowered variety grows near Geraldton. It occurs from Kalbarri to the Fitzgerald River.

## The Sundew Family — Droseraceae

Plants belonging to this family are all annual or perennial herbs. The family is best known for having species with leaves covered in glandular insect-trapping hairs. There are four genera only one of which occurs in Western Australia.

### *Drosera*

Sundews are generally delicate herbs with sticky hairs on their leaves. All species are predatory, catching insect prey. A few kinds are known from Europe and North America, but the majority of the world's sundews are found in south-west Australia. Many have a rosette of leaves on the ground, others have erect stems or are creepers up to 2 m tall. Mostly they have attractive flowers coloured pink, white or yellow. About 45 species are found in Western Australia.

**Pimpernel Sundew, *D. glanduligera,*** is a widespread rosette species with orange flowers.

**Indian Sundew, *D. indica,*** is the main species found in the north from Kalbarri to Queensland. It is also widely distributed from Africa to Japan.

**Bridal Rainbow, *D. macrantha,*** is a common climbing species in the south-west with pink or white flowers. The similar *D. pallida* has white flowers.

**Pink Rainbow, *D. menziesii,*** is a delicate, trailing plant with pink flowers, which grows over rocks and in damp places.

## The Violet Family — Violaceae

There are about 800 species in the family, mainly found in north temperate regions and on tropical mountains.

### *Hybanthus*
Perennial herbs or shrubs including about 150 species distributed in the Americas, South Africa, Asia and Australia. Eight occur in Western Australia.

**Wild Violet, *H. calycinus,*** extends from Kalbarri to near Augusta.

## The Caper Family — Capparaceae

A family (sometimes spelt Capparidaceae) of mainly shrubs and small trees often with attractive flowers. They grow in all tropical regions of the world with 25 species in Australia.

**Coastal Caper, *Capparis spinosa,*** is a common shrub up to 1 m tall with rounded leaves, which grows mainly along rocky coasts in the Pilbara and Kimberley. It has large white flowers with long stamens.

**Pink Cleome, *Cleome oxalidea,*** grows in low-lying areas near rivers and streams in the north-west. It flowers profusely after summer rains.

## The Australian Heath Family — Epacridaceae

This family is largely restricted to Australia, with a few species in South-east Asia, Indonesia, and New Zealand. One is found in South America. The plants have a superficial resemblance to heathers (Ericaceae), often having tubular flowers and a shrubby habit. There are more than 130 species in Western Australia, with several genera not found anywhere else.

### *Andersonia*
Generally rather lavender-like bushes with mauve flowers. There are about 22 species, all restricted to the south-west.

***A. lehmaniana*** grows mainly in the Darling Range, extending from Jurien Bay to south of Perth.

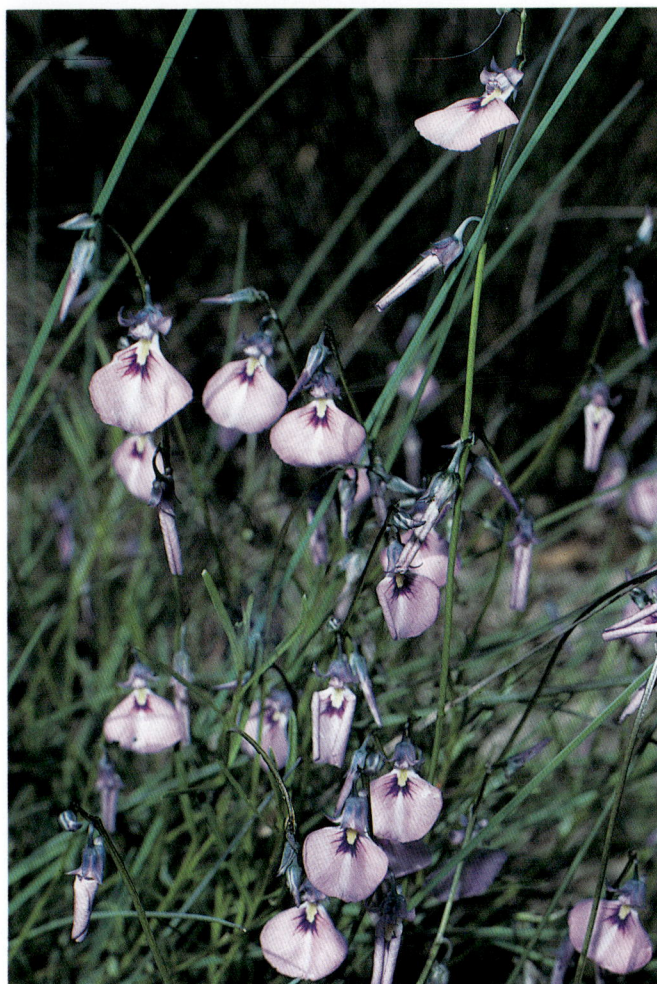

*Hybanthus calycinus* (Jul.-Oct.)

**Giant Andersonia, *A. axilliflora,*** is a 'monkey-puzzle'-like bush which grows on the Stirling Range with cream coloured leaves around its flowers.

### *Astroloma*
Mostly low, prickly, heather-like shrubs with white or red flowers. There are 18 species recognized in Western Australia.

**Moss-Leaved Heath, *A. ciliatum,*** has a mat-like growth-form with purple or red flowers.

***A. glaucescens,*** one of the more striking species, is found between Geraldton and Perth growing on both sands and gravels.

### *Conostephium*
An endemic genus with five known species in the south-west.

**Pearl Flower, *C. pendulum,*** is commonly found near Perth.

### *Leucopogon*
These plants are known as the beard-heaths, because they have hairs within the flower. This is a large genus with 71 species found in Western Australia. They usually have sharp-pointed leaves and smallish, white flowers.

**Nodding Leucopogon, *L. nutans,*** has many pendulous flowers. It flowers in May-June and can be found inland from

*Leucopogon nutans* (May-Jun.) *(ABOVE)*
*Sollya heterophylla* (Oct.-Feb.) *(RIGHT)*

Jurien Bay to near Walpole on the south coast.

**Tassel Flower, *L. verticillatus,*** is an atypical species with rings of large leaves and tassels of flowers. It is found mainly in the Karri forest, but does extend as far as Perth in the Jarrah forest.

### *Lysinema*
These are spindly erect shrubs with long flowers at the end of tall stalks.

**Curry Flower, *L. ciliatum,*** is the most commonly seen. It is found from Kalbarri south, and east to the Nullarbor Plain.

### *Sphenotoma*
Paper heaths have paper-like flowers. All of the six known species are restricted to the south-west.

**Paper Heath, *S. dracophylloides,*** is an erect shrub which grows on the Stirling Range and near Albany on the south coast.

## The Pittosporum Family — Pittosporaceae

The family contains about 200 species, mainly in warm temperate areas. It is well represented in Australia, Africa, Asia and New Zealand. They are mainly trees or shrubs, but include many climbers. There are three species of *Pittosporum* found in Western Australia, all small trees with yellowish fruits.

### *Billardiera*
These are vines with brightly coloured flowers. They may have red, orange, white, cream or mauve flowers. There are 17 species altogether in Western Australia.

**Red Billardiera, *B. erubescens,*** occurs in inland areas of the south-west, and the Stirling Range.

### *Sollya*
These vines have attractive blue flowers, and are known as Australian bluebells. Three species are known in Western Australia.

**Australian Bluebell, *S. heterophylla,*** has a bush-like growth-form, or can be a twining climber. It is widespread in the south-west from north of Perth to Esperance.

## The Rainbow Plant Family — Byblidaceae

These are insectivorous herbs somewhat like the sundews. Only four species are known — two occurring in South Africa and two in Australia. The family is represented by the genus *Byblis* with two species.

**The Giant Rainbow Plant, *B. gigantea,*** is found in wet depressions from Perth to north of Jurien Bay.

**Northern Rainbow, *B. liniflora,*** is widespread in tropical Australia.

## The Albany Pitcherplant Family — Cephalotaceae

This family is only represented by one unique plant. Its flowers place it close to the Saxifrage family.

**Albany Pitcher Plant, *Cephalotus follicularis,*** is restricted to the south coast region between Albany and Augusta. It grows in swampy conditions and has rosettes of leaves with pitchers for catching insects. The pitchers which this plant has evolved are remarkably similar to those of other, unrelated pitcher plants.

## The Wattle Family — Mimosaceae

The wattle family is well adapted to living in arid conditions, usually having phyllodes instead of leaves to reduce water loss. Characteristically the plants have spherical or oblong puffball-like flower-heads, usually yellow, but some white, green or pink. The seeds are held in pea-like pods, the families being related. Like peas and beans, wattles have root nodules with nitrogen-fixing bacteria, so the plants can improve soil fertility. This facility also makes them nutrient rich, so they attract many insects. There are over 3000 species, mainly found in warmer countries, especially those with arid or semi-arid climates. Most are trees or shrubs, but some are herbs.

### *Acacia*
The wattles form an important part of the West Australian vegetation, occurring in most areas. They are the dominant shrub in the mulga zone of the arid interior, varying in size from woody plants 50 cm high to small trees. They differ from the wattles typical of Africa in that they do not have rapier-like thorns, although there are exceptions. Many Australian species have prickly points at the end of their leaves. There are over 500 species in the west and more are being described each year. Only a few species can be included here, because of limited space.

*Acacia drummondii* (Jul.-Oct.) (ABOVE)
*Acacia hamersleyensis* (Jul.-Aug.) (RIGHT)

**Jam Tree, *A. acuminata*,** has an umbrella-like growth-form and is very common in the Wheatbelt area. The leaves have curved ends.

**Mulga, *A. aneura*,** is often the dominant species in the semi-arid mulga zone. It is a very variable shrub, well adapted to the arid region. The severe drought of the last ice age is likely to have isolated many populations so that the varieties were in the process of evolving into new species.

**Drummond's Wattle, *A. drummondii*,** has pinnate leaves and grows up to 2 m with masses of elongated flowerheads. It is mainly found in the Stirling Range and Albany area, but does occur further north.

**Mimosa Bush, *A. farnesiana*,** has spines and mainly grows in the north. It comes from Central America and is used in the perfume trade. It was probably brought in by the Portuguese before Captain Cook came to Australia. Mesquite from America also has spines and occurs as a weed in the Pilbara region.

***A. hamersleyensis*** is an attractive species with a very restricted range in the Pilbara.

***A. lasiocalyx*** is often seen growing along roadsides in Wheatbelt areas. It has 20 cm long leaves.

**Karri Wattle, *A. pentadenia*,** has cream-coloured flowers and pinnate leaves. It grows up to 5 m tall, and is found in the Jarrah and Karri areas of the far south-west.

**Prickly Moses** (the name comes from *Mimosa*), ***A. pulchella*,** is a dense bush with needle-like spines and pinnate leaves. It is possible that this spiny species is a relatively recent immigrant, perhaps coming to Australia during one of the ice ages.

**Orange Wattle, *A. saligna*,** grows into a small tree. It is the common wattle in Perth and extends throughout the south-west from Kalbarri to Israelite Bay.

**Kurara, *A. tetragonophylla*,** is a common species in the semi-arid zone, it has very spiny leaves.

Other arid zone species include the dark, shady Gidgee trees and five kinds of minni ritchi bushes, which have unique curly red bark.

## *Neptunia*
This includes species of sensitive plant. Two are known in Western Australia, mainly growing in the Kimberley but also extending into the Pilbara.

**Sensitive Plant, *N. monosperma*,** has a ground-creeping habit and yellow flowers. The leaves close if the plant is touched.

## *Paraseriathes*
Formerly known as *Albizia*. Three species are known in Western Australia.

***P. lophantha*** is a fast-growing small tree up to about 10 m high, with large greenish, tassel-like flowers and dense clusters of seed pods. It is widespread in damp areas in the Darling Scarp down to the south coast. It occurs in Indonesia and has been introduced into eastern Australia and South Africa.

# The Cassia Family — Cuoualpinaceae

This family is related to the wattles. The plants usually have yellow-petalled flowers and large seed pods. Several species are grown in gardens, such as Indian Laburnum, *Cassia fistula*. Most occur in the Kimberley and Pilbara regions and semi-arid areas, except for the hibbertia-like *Labichea punctata*, which occurs in the Perth area.

## *Cassia*
There are 23 species found in the West.

**The Cockroach Bush, *C. notabilis*,** is a well-known species which grows along roadsides in the Pilbara. Its seedpods look like cockroaches.

***C. venusta*** is a showy species which grows along watercourses in the Pilbara and Kimberley districts.

# The Pea Family — Papilionaceae

This is another very important family in Australia. One of the reasons for its abundance may be the poverty of Australian soils. Wattles and peas cope well because they are able to produce their own nitrogenous fertilizers using root nodules. The family is characterised by its unusual flowers, with petals divided into the upper wing petal and the lower keel which wraps around the stamens and

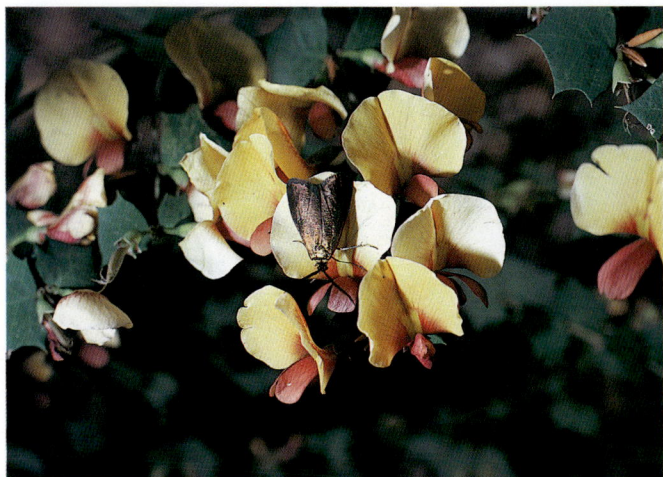

*Bossiaea aquilifolium* (Aug.-Sep.)

stigma. Like the previous families, the seeds are held in a pod. Worldwide there are over 12,000 species, many important food crops and fodder species. Many grow into trees, such as the flame tree, *Erythrina*, which is grown in cities — *E. vespertilio* is a related species which grows naturally in the north. Other northern trees include the White Dragon Tree, *Sesbania formosa*. The family contains 52 genera in the West. A selection is shown here to indicate the great variety of forms present.

## Bossiaea
Typically these are dense bushes with yellow and brown flowers. There are about 40 species in Australia with 20 in the West.

**Holly-leaved Bossiaea, *B. aquilifolium*,** grows on lateritic soils in the Darling Range near Perth and south to Bunbury and Collie. It is a dense prickly bush up to 2.5 m high.

## Burtonia
A genus of about 12 species, ten in the West.

**Painted Lady, *B. scabra*,** is found from north of Perth to the South Coast. *B. villosa* is a similar species only found in the Stirling Range National Park.

## Clianthus

**Sturt Pea, *C. formosus*,** was first collected by William Dampier in 1699. It grows mainly on dry stream beds, or flat areas subject to occasional inundation. It is found from North-west Cape and the arid interior to the Nullarbor Plain, also across Australia to New South Wales. The flowers may be seen June-September, and are interesting because they are pollinated by birds.

## Crotalaria
These shrubs mainly have yellow flowers and grow in the north of Australia.

**Green Bird Flower, *C. cunninghamii*,** has large greenish flowers and grows up to about 2 m tall, often near roadsides in the north.

## Daviesia
Usually dense prickly bushes with small red or orange flowers. The genus is endemic to Australia, with 90 of the 110 species

found in Western Australia.

***D. hakeoides*** mainly occurs in the inland south-west, and has several subspecies.

## Gastrolobium
This is another genus which has yellow-and-brown flowers. All members contain the poison monofluoroacetate and are toxic to stock. Native animals and birds are largely immune to the poison, and the chemical is widely used for the control of foxes, rabbits and other introduced pests. There are 47 species in all, 45 of them in Western Australia.

**York Road Poison, *G. calycinum*,** was the first to be recognized as being poisonous. It grows in the Darling Range and further inland.

**Lamb's Poison, *Isotropis cuneifolia*.** *Isotropis* is one of several other genera with similar yellow-and-brown flowers, which also include *Gompholobium*, *Nemcia* and *Oxylobium*.

## Hardenbergia

**Native Wistaria or Sarsaparilla, *H. comptoniana*,** is a vigorous climber with deep mauve flowers. It grows from Jurien Bay to Albany. Two other species occur in Australia.

## Hovea
These bushes have purple flowers, and are among the first flowering shrubs to be noticed in early spring. There are six species in the West.

**Common Hovea, *H. trisperma*,** occurs from Geraldton to the South Coast.

**Devil's Pins, *H. pungens*,** has sharp pointed leaves and is more local, with some found near Perth, Jurien Bay, near Kalgoorlie and Esperance.

## Kennedia
This genus is well known for the Coral Vine, *K. coccinea*. Black Kennedia, *K. nigricans*, is also grown in gardens. It is a strong vine, which grows near the south coast, especially near the Fitzgerald River National Park. It has black flowers with a yellow throat and is much visited by honeyeaters. There are 11 species in the genus altogether.

**Scarlet Runner, *K. prostrata*,** is a widespread ground-creeping plant in the south-west.

## Swainsona
This is an important genus in the north and arid areas. The plants often grow in profusion at the roadside after heavy rain.

**The Ashburton Pea, *S. macullochiana*,** is a tall, showy species found in the Ashburton Fortescue district in the Pilbara.

***S. forrestii*** is found inland from Carnarvon.

## Templetonia

**Cockies' Tongues, *T. retusa*,** is a dense, dark-leaved bush with masses of red flowers in winter. It grows well on coastal limestone from Kalbarri to Israelite Bay. Ten other species are found in Western Australia.

*Hovea pungens* (Jun.-Nov.) *(LEFT)*
*Swainsona forrestii* *(ABOVE)*

## The Banksia Family — Proteaceae

This family is well-known for the South African proteas. Usually shrubs or trees, the species are found mainly in South Africa and Australia, with a few also present in South America and from China to New Zealand. There are over 1000 species in all, with nearly 500 occurring in Western Australia, mainly in the south-west.

### Adenanthos

Includes Woolly Bush, *A. cygnorum*, which grows up to 4 m tall and extends from Kalbarri to Collie. It has green flowers. A similar species with red flowers occurs on the south coast. About 20 species are known, most from Western Australia.

**Basket Flower, *A. obovatus*,** is a small shrub with bright red flower spikes which grows near swamp margins from south of Jurien Bay to Albany.

### Banksia

Well known for its cone-like flowers and seed heads. The genus is confined to Australia (one species does extend into New Guinea). There are a total of 72 species, of which 59 are found in the West. The majority are confined to the south-west. They range in size from those with underground creeping stems to 12 m tall trees. The cones are an adaptation to fire — most banksias are killed by fire, but the cones store seed, which is released soon after a fire sweeps through. Near Perth the common banksia trees are the brownish *B. menziesii* and yellow-flowered *B. attenuata*. Others include *B. grandis* and *B. prionotes* mentioned below. *B. speciosa* is the common species along roadsides near the south coast between

the Fitzgerald River and Israelite Bay.

**Ashby's Banksia, *B. ashbyi*,** has the most northerly distribution, extending from south of Geraldton to North-west Cape. It grows to about 5 m tall and its orange flowers can be seen from August to January.

**Brown's Banksia, *B. brownii*,** is one of several species with very restricted distributions. This one occurs on mountains in the Stirling Range. Like most of the Proteaceae it is very susceptible to die-back fungus, and is under threat as the pathogen spreads through the park.

**Scarlet Banksia, *B. coccinea*,** grows as a slender, stiff-leaved bush capped by squat scarlet flowers, in the Stirling Ranges and along the south coast to the Fitzgerald River.

**Red Swamp Banksia, *B. occidentalis*,** is another red species growing near the south coast. It forms dense bushes with pliable leaves.

**Bull Banksia, *B. grandis*,** grows as an understorey tree up to 10 m tall in the Jarrah forest. It has large, dark-green leaves and tall, cream flowers. It occurs from Jurien Bay to east of Albany on the south coast.

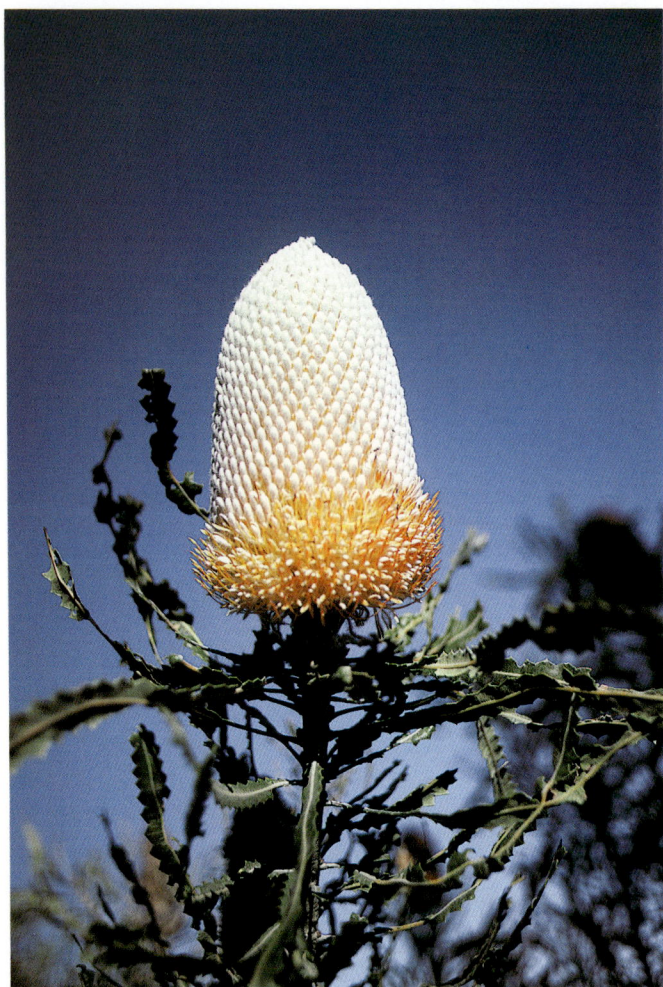

*Banksia coccinea* (Jun.-Oct.) *(RIGHT)*
*Banksia prionotes* (Mar.-May) *(ABOVE)*

**Nodding Banksia, *B. nutans,*** forms a dense bush with needle-like leaves and has brown flowers which hang from the branches. Several species have nodding flowers like this and grow in areas where pollination by mammals is important — especially the Honey Possum.

This banksia is common on heaths from the Stirling Range to Esperance.

**Acorn Banksia, *B. prionotes,*** is one of the most spectacular species, with bushes often covered with bright orange flowers. It extends from Perth to Shark Bay, and east to Wagin.

**Creeping Banksia, *B. repens,*** and the similar *B. prostrata* have creeping underground stems with only the leaves and flowers above ground. They grow in heathy areas near the south coast which are subject to frequent fires. They have adopted this habit in order to survive — most other banksias are killed by fire.

## *Conospermum*

These plants are known as smoke bushes because they have masses of woolly flowers which appear to hover over the bushes. Some species grow up to 2 m tall, and most have white woolly hairs, but some are blue or pink. Forty species are known, of which 29 occur in Western Australia.

**Common Smokebush, *C. stoechadis,*** grows mainly on sandy soils from Shark Bay to near the Stirling Range.

## *Dryandra*

This is another very large genus of plants with somewhat banksia-like flowers and prickly leaves. There are 60 species, all of which are restricted to Western Australia.

**Pingle, *D. carduacea,*** is a prickly shrub up to 3 m high with long, erect branches covered in flowers. It grows on heavier soils and extends from near Geraldton to within 100 km of the Stirling Range.

**Couch Honeypot, *D. nivea,*** is one of the prostrate species with brown, nectar-dripping flowers on the ground. It is adapted to pollination by Honey Possums, and occurs from near Geraldton to Esperance.

**Parrot Bush, *D. sessilis,*** grows as a holly-like bush up to 5 m tall. It is a prolific seeder and grows into dense stands after fires. It flowers all year and provides a reliable source of nectar for honeyeaters, which often nest near these bushes. Parrots and bronzewing pigeons eat the seeds. It ranges from Kalbarri in the north to east of Albany on the south coast.

## *Grevillea*

These are often very showy shrubs, many of which are grown in gardens. The Silky Oak, *G. robusta* is a tree from New South Wales. There are 250 species altogether, with 150 found in Western Australia. They occur throughout the region, with some species adapted to living in the arid interior. The flowers vary in colour, but are mainly white, orange or red.

**Bipinnate Grevillea, *G. bipinnatifida,*** is a low shrub up to 1 m with pale, reddish flowers. It is found in the northern part of the Jarrah forest and is often grown in gardens.

**Flame Grevillea, *G. eriostachya,*** has pale yellow flowers and grows to about 6 m tall. It grows on sandy heathland in the Wheatbelt area. A related species, *G. excelsior*, has orange flowers.

**White Plume Grevillea, *G. leucopteris,*** grows into a dense bush and has flower stems 2 m above the foliage to attract birds. It is often planted along roadsides in the city, but its strong, somewhat sickly scent deters some gardeners. Its natural range is in sand heaths between Geraldton and Kalbarri.

**Wilson's Grevillea, *G. wilsonii,*** is a prickly bush with bright red flowers found in the Jarrah forest.

## *Hakea*

Usually prickly shrubs with white flowers or leathery-leaved, small

*Dryandra carduacea* (Jul.-Nov.) *(ABOVE)*
*Grevillea bipinnatifida* (Mar.-Nov.) *(RIGHT)*

trees with pink or red flowers. They all have woody, nut-like seed capsules (fruit) to protect the seeds from fire. The capsule opens soon after fire has passed, releasing two winged seeds. Cricket Ball Hakea, *H. platysperma*, has 6 cm diameter capsules. Pincushion Hakea, *H. laurina*, which has spherical flowerheads, is often grown in gardens. 150 species are known of which over 100 are from Western Australia. They are mainly concentrated in the south-west, but some are adapted to hot, arid areas, including some in the Kimberley region.

**Pink Spike Hakea, *H. coriacea*,** grows into a tree up to 7 m tall and has conspicuous pink or red flower spikes and long, flat leaves. It grows on gravel east of Geraldton to Southern Cross.

**Honeybush, *H. lissocarpha*,** is generally a small bush up to 1.5 m tall. It has masses of white flowers in early spring with a strong, sweet scent. It is found in forest and heathlands from Kalbarri to the south coast.

**Royal Hakea, *H. victoriae*,** is a spectacular species restricted to the Fitzgerald River National Park.

## Isopogon
This genus is closely allied to *Petrophile*, which is included here. They both have species with flowers grouped into a head and seeds in a cone-like structure. They are generally woody bushes with

conspicuous pink or cream-coloured flowers. There are 25 species of *Isopogon* in Western Australia, and 33 of *Petrophile*.

**Pincushion Coneflower, *I. dubius*,** has flowerheads, which look rather like thistles. It grows in the northern part of the Jarrah forest.

**Barrel Coneflower, *I. trilobus*,** is conspicuous with its silver, barrel-like cones. It grows on heaths near the south coast, east of Albany.

***I. latifolius*** is a fine species which grows on the peaks in the Stirling Range. Large areas have been killed by die-back fungus.

**Pixie Mops, *Petrophile linearis*,** is common on the coastal plain in the Perth area, extending from Jurien Bay to Augusta.

## Lambertia
These shrubs usually have terminal clusters of seven cream or orange flowers. There are ten species, nine of which grow in the south-west.

**Chittick, *L. inermis*,** is a slender, straggly bush with clusters of orange, or sometimes cream, flowers. It bears flowers most of the year, occurring near the south coast from Albany to Israelite Bay. *L. ericifolia* is similar but has heather-like leaves.

## Persoonia
This genus of trees and shrubs ranges as far as New Zealand. The flowers are usually yellow and are followed by succulent fruits,

*Hakea coriacea* (Jul.-Sep.) *(TOP LEFT)*
*Isopogon latifolius* *(TOP RIGHT)*
*Petrophile linearis* (Sep.-Nov.) *(ABOVE)*
*Xylomelum angustifolium* (Dec.-Jan.) *(RIGHT)*

from which the plants get their unattractive name snottygobble. There are 75 species with 28 in Western Australia.

**Broad-leaved Snottygobble, *P. elliptica*,** is a small tree found in the Jarrah forest. *P. longifolia* has narrow leaves and is more common further south in the Karri

forest. Both have fire-resistant bark.

## Synaphea

These are small shrubs, most of which have many tall spikes of yellow flowers sprouting above the leaves. There are about ten species, all confined to Western Australia.

**Graceful Synaphea, *S. gracillima*,** is found from near Perth to the south coast.

## Xylomelum

These are known as woody pears, because of their large, pear-shaped fruit which contain two winged seeds like those of hakeas. They are small trees up to 8 m tall. There are four species, two in Western Australia.

**Woody Pear, *X. occidentale*,** in found from Perth to Augusta. It has large holly-like leaves and grows to 8 m tall.

**Sandplain Woody Pear, *X. angustifolium*,** is a smaller, more graceful shrub which grows on heaths from east of the Darling Range to Kalbarri.

## The Water Milfoil Family — Haloragaceae

Includes mainly aquatic or terrestrial herbs. There are eight genera with about 100 species, mainly concentrated in Australia. Water milfoils, *Myriophyllum*, have finely divided leaves and are often grown in aquaria. There are 17 milfoils in Western Australia.

### Glischrocaryon

These are erect perennial herbs with terminal flowerheads. They are restricted to Australia, with three of the four known species occurring in Western Australia.

**Common Popflower, *G. aureum*,** often grows in disturbed soil along roadsides and in gravel pits. It is widespread from Kalbarri to the south coast, and inland to Kalgoorlie.

*Pimelia spectabilis* (Sep.-Nov.) *(BELOW)*
*Pimelia suaveolens* (Jun.-Oct.) *(RIGHT)*

## The Banjine Family — Thymeliaceae

Usually shrubs or trees with a very stringy bark, which is sometimes used for making rope. The leaves are simple and entire, and the flowers are usually tubular. There are about 500 species in tropical and temperate regions, with most concentrated in Africa.

### Pimelia

This is the only genus found in Western Australia, where there are 45 species. It includes the very attractive banjines, which are often grown in gardens. There are about 100 species altogether distributed through Australia and New Zealand. They include the unusual Qualup Bell, *P. physodes*, which looks like a kind of *Darwinia* (Myrtaceae), and the Cream Banjine, *P. clavata*, which grows up to 3 m tall in the Karri forest.

***P. ferruginea*** grows as an erect shrub up to 1 m tall with many pink flowerheads. It grows mainly on coastal dunes from near Geraldton to Esperance.

**Bunjong, *P. spectabilis*,** grows up to 2 m tall with erect branches supporting many pink or white flowerheads. It is mainly found on lateritic soils in the Darling Range near Perth and from Augusta to Albany.

**Scented Banjine, *P. suaveolens*,** is usually a many-stemmed bush with pendant yellow flowers in winter or early spring. Its range extends from Jurien Bay to the Stirling Range and east to near Kalgoorlie.

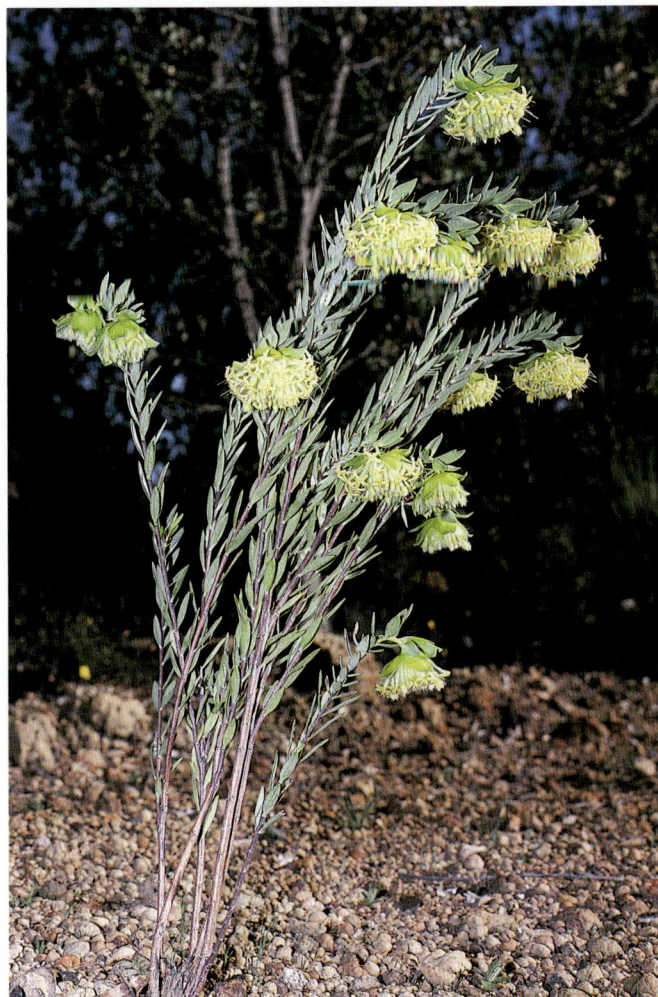

# The Eucalyptus Family — Myrtaceae

This is one of the major plant families in Australia and includes many genera, with species ranging from small undershrubs to some of the largest trees in the world. The leaves are usually aromatic and the fruit a woody capsule. The family includes about 3500 species, which are concentrated mainly in the tropics and southern temperate regions, especially in Australia and South America.

## *Agonis*

Shrubs or small trees with flowers in clusters on the branches. Ten species, all confined to Western Australia, include the Peppermint, *A. flexuosa*, which is a common weeping tree up to 15 m tall found mainly in coastal areas from Perth to the east of Albany. Warren River Cedar, *A. juniperina*, is an attractive tree which grows in swamps and along river banks in the extreme south-west.

**Arnica, *A. marginata*,** grows on granite hills near the south coast at Albany.

## *Astartea, Baeckea, Scholtzia*

These are three somewhat similar groups, which are usually covered in many five-petalled pink or white flowers. There are about 8 species of *Astartea*, 20 of *Baeckea* and 15 of *Scholtzia*. All of them are confined to the south-west.

**Camphor Myrtle, *Baeckea camphorosmae*,** is a small spreading shrub which flowers mainly in late spring and summer. It ranges from Jurien Bay to Albany.

***Scholtzia capitata*** is a woody shrub up to 1.5 m tall, which becomes smothered in small pink flowers during September. It grows on sandy gravel in the Wheatbelt, east of Perth.

## *Beaufortia*

One of the many groups of bottlebrushes. There are 17 species all confined to the south-west.

**Swamp Bottlebrush, *B. sparsa*,** has conspicuous orange-red flowers, which add much colour to swamps near the south coast. It flowers mainly during the summer.

## *Callistemon*

This is the group, which provides most of the bottlebrushes grown in gardens. There are about 30 species mainly found in eastern Australia. Only two are found in the West.

**Albany Bottlebrush, *C. speciosus*,** mainly grows on swamp margins near the south coast and extends north into the Jarrah forest.

## *Calothamnus*

These are known as one-sided bottlebrushes. The flowers are generally arranged with the main colour coming from bundled stamens. There are about 35 species, all confined to the south-west.

**Mouse Ears, *C. rupestris*,** grows to about 3 m tall on a few granite rocks east of Perth.

## *Calytrix*

These are known as starflowers because most species have five points and the sepals have long, persistent awns. They are usually small shrubs with yellow or purple flowers.

**Starflower, *C. glutinosa*,** extends from near Geraldton to east of Perth. It mainly grows near granitic rocks.

## *Chamelaucium*

Shrubs in this genus usually have well developed flowers with five broad petals. There are about 23 species, all restricted to the south-west.

**Geraldton Wax, *C. uncinatum*,** is widely grown in gardens. It occurs naturally from Perth to Kalbarri.

## *Darwinia*

Characteristically these plants have bell-like flowers which are in fact flowerheads inside petal-like bracts. There are about 60 species, with 46 in the south-west. The Stirling Range mountain tops have a number of spectacular, endemic species.

**Mountain Bell, *D. leiostyla*,** is one of the more widespread species in the Stirling Range.

## *Eremaea*

Bushy, somewhat hairy shrubs with small, dense bottlebrush flowerheads. There are 15 species, which are all endemic to Western Australia.

***E. pauciflora*** has attractive orange flowers, and grows mainly on sandy areas from Jurien Bay south and east to near Kalgoorlie.

## *Eucalyptus*

These are the characteristic trees of Australia. They range from shrub-like mallees to trees up to 80 m high. They have opposite juvenile leaves and usually alternate, strap-like mature leaves. The flowers have an operculum, which drops off when the flower opens. The seeds are held in a fire-resistant nut. There are about 500 species, which are almost entirely restricted to Australia. Over 200 are found in Western Australia. Some of the more important species are described in the section on vegetation.

**River Gum, *E. camaldulensis*.** This is an attractive, white-barked tree, which grows along rivers in the north. It is a variable species with a wide distribution, extending into eastern Australia. The Flooded Gum, *E. rudis*, which grows in the south-west is closely allied to it.

**West Australian Coolabah, *E. microtheca*,** grows in similar locations to the River Gum in the Pilbara and Kimberley, but prefers less permanent water, especially temporary swamps and ephemeral streams. Other similar white-barked species in the north include the Ghost Gum, *E. papuana*, which occurs in the Kimberley district and eastern desert regions.

**Mottlecah, *E. macrocarpa*.** This tree has a mallee growth form and large silvery leaves. It also has 10 cm flowers, which are the largest of all gum trees. It grows on sandheaths from Jurien Bay in the north to inland areas near Lake Grace.

**Illyarrie, *E. erythrocorys*,** has large yellow flowers and grows on coastal hills near Jurien Bay, south of Geraldton.

## *Hypocalymma*

Attractive scented bushes generally known as myrtles. There are about 14 species all confined to the south-west.

**Swan River Myrtle, *H. robustum*,** is often grown in

*Hypocalymma robustum* (Jul.-Oct.) *(TOP)*
*Calothamnus rupestris* (Jul.-Nov.) *(ABOVE)*
*Eremaea pauciflora* (Sep.-Nov.) *(RIGHT)*

gardens. It grows on sandplain and laterite from near Perth to the Karri forest.

**White Myrtle, *H. angustifolium*,** is common in swampy areas from Geraldton to Albany.

## Kunzea
Another group with bottlebrush flowers. There are about 24 species altogether, with 13 in Western Australia. They may have green, cream or red flowers.

**Baxter's Bottlebrush, *K. baxteri*,** which is often grown in gardens, grows naturally only on granite outcrops near Esperance.

## Leptospermum
Superficially similar to *Chamelaucium* these are widespread shrubs or small trees with over 70 species extending as far as south-east Asia and New Zealand. Nine species are native to Western Australia.

**Tea tree, *L. erubescens*,** grows on laterite in the Darling Range.

## Melaleuca
A large, mainly Australian genus of trees and shrubs, often with white, pink, or sometimes red, bottlebrush flowers. They include paperbark trees which are typical of swampland in the south-west,

particularly *M. raphiophylla* in fresh water and *M. cuticularis* in saline swamps. There are over 150 species with more than 120 in Western Australia.

**Robin Redbreast Bush, *M. lateritia*,** has showy red flowers and grows in winter-wet depressions between Jurien Bay and Albany.

**Rough Honeymyrtle, *M. scabra*,** grows mainly in gravel soils from Shark Bay to Israelite Bay.

### *Regelia*
Unusual rigidly upright shrubs up to 3 m tall, with dense opposite leaves. There are about 6 species known, all from the south-west.

**Barrens Regelia, *R. velutina*,** grows only on quartzite rocks in the Barrens Range in the Fitzgerald River National Park.

### *Verticordia*
These are known as featherflowers, and are usually low shrubs with densely packed feathery flowers. There are about 60 species occurring in the south-west and in the north; almost all are restricted to Western Australia. Their flowers are particularly spectacular in late spring in the Lake Grace-Lake King area.

**Yellow Featherflower, *V. chrysantha*,** is relatively widespread in the inland south-west.

## The Sandalwood Family — Santalaceae

These plants range from herbs to small trees. All are semi-parasites with haustorial roots attaching themselves onto host plants. About 400 species are known in the world. In Western Australia the family includes Broom Ballart, *Exocarpus sparteus*, which is a weeping, broom-like shrub often seen at the roadsides in the south-west, and about 13 species of currant bushes, such as *Leptomeria cunninghamii*, which is a small shrub with masses of minute brown flowers.

### *Santalum*
Trees or shrubs with somewhat succulent leathery leaves, which are restricted to Australia, Indonesia and Oceania. About 25 species are known, with four occurring in Western Australia.

**Sweet Quandong, *S. acuminatum*,** is a dense tree up to 5 m high with round, red fruit and a large, rugose nut. It occurs over most of Australia and grows along the coast as far north as Carnarvon, as well as in the arid interior.

**Sandalwood, *S. spicatum*,** is similar to the Quandong, but is more rigid and has a smooth nut. It is widespread in inland areas. The wood is scented and exported to Asia.

## The Mistletoe Family — Loranthaceae

Leathery evergreen trees or shrubs often with sticky, succulent fruit. They are semi-parasites on other plants. Over 700 species are known, mainly in the tropics.

### *Amyema* and *Lysiana*
Formerly known as *Loranthus*. The seeds of these parasites are distributed by the Mistletoebird, which feeds on the fruit, and wipes the sticky seeds onto branches where it perches. There are 24 species known from Western Australia.

**Stalked Mistletoe, *A. miquelii*,** commonly grows on gum trees, where its leaves look remarkably gum-like.

### *Nuytsia*

**Christmas Tree, *N. floribunda*.** This species is unique to Western Australia. It grows up to 8 m tall and has an abundance of orange-gold flowers, mainly in the period December-January. The seeds are three-winged and unusual in not being fleshy. It is found from Kalbarri to Israelite Bay.

## The Giant Flower Family — Rafflesiaceae

This family includes the largest flower in the world, *Rafflesia*, which grows in Indonesia and Malaysia. The plants are parasitic.

***Pilostyles hamiltonii*** is one of two species which occur in Western Australia. It is a parasite of *Jacksonia* and *Daviesia* (Papilionaceae), and its small red flowers can be seen emerging from the stems of these plants in late summer and autumn.

## Stackhousia Family — Stackhousiaceae

These are mainly herbaceous plants, which are restricted to Australia, New Zealand, Indonesia and adjacent islands. Only about 25 species are known.

### *Stackhousia*
Mainly erect annual or perennial herbs with spikes of fragrant yellow or white flowers. Fourteen species are known with about eight in Western Australia.

***S. monogyna*** is widespread in the south-west from near Kalbarri to Israelite Bay and near Kalgoorlie.

## The Spurge Family — Euphorbiaceae

A large family well-known in the garden for *Poinsettia* and the weed, Petty Spurge. The family includes the tree from which rubber is made. Many members of the family produce a milky latex, which deters caterpillars and protects the leaves from insects. The family has a worldwide distribution with about 7500 species known.

### *Phyllanthus*
A widespread genus of herbs, shrubs and small trees. Most are found in the north of Australia, with 14 species in Western Australia.

***P. calycinus*** is the only species which extends into the south-west. It is found from Kalbarri to Israelite Bay.

## The Buckthorn Family — Rhamnaceae

Mainly trees and shrubs including the European buckthorns, *Rhamnus*. The family is widespread, with over 900 species.

### *Cryptandra*
Low shrubs which are often hairy, and some are spiny. Forty species are found in temperate Australia with 23 occurring in Western Australia.

**Spiny Cryptandra, *C. pungens*,** is widespread in the south-west from Geraldton to Israelite Bay.

### *Trymalium*
Hairy shrubs or small trees, with about 11 species known, of which

*Amyema miquelii* (Mar.-Jul.) *(ABOVE)*
*Trymalium ledifolium* (Jul.-Oct.) *(RIGHT)*

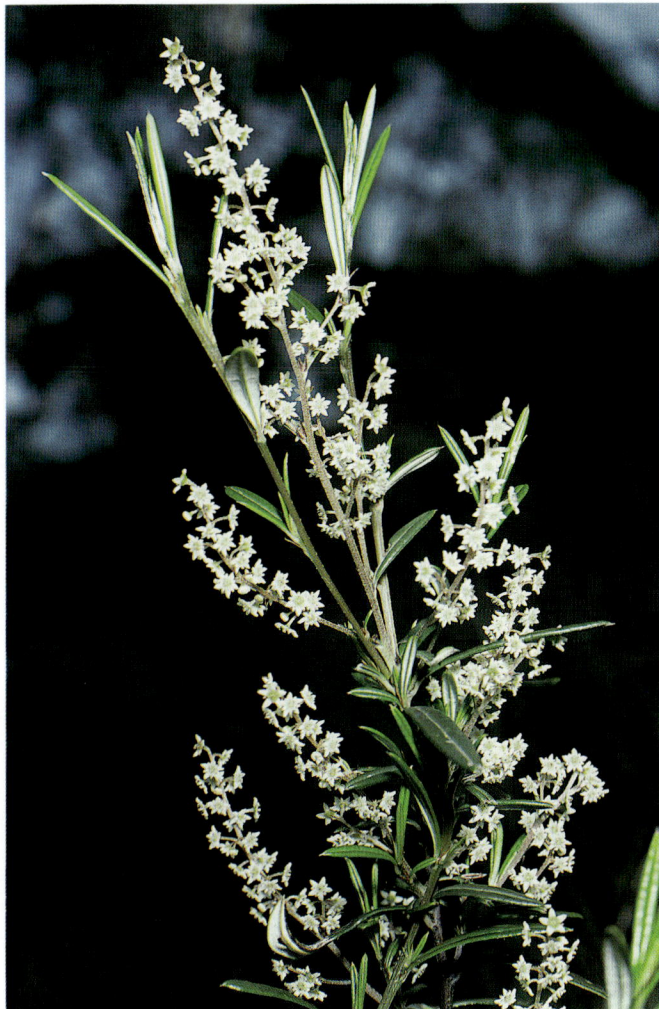

seven are found in Western Australia.

**Karri Hazel, *T. floribundum*** (also known as *T. spath-ulatum*), has broad, hazel-like juvenile leaves, becoming narrower as the tree grows taller. They may grow up to 10 m high in the Karri forest, but usually remain as small bushes near Perth.

***T. ledifolium*** is a more common and widespread species, extending from Jurien Bay to Albany.

## The Tremandra Family — Tremandraceae

This is another family which is endemic to Australia. There are 43 species known, mainly small shrubs with conspicuous pink or violet flowers.

### *Platytheca*
Only two species are known, both restricted to the south-west.

***P. galioides*** is a low, fine-leaved, woody plant with deep purple flowers, which face the ground. It grows in damp situations near the coast from Jurien Bay to near Albany.

***P. juniperina*** is a woody shrub with sharp-pointed leaves. It

only occurs on peaks in the Stirling Range and Barrens.

### *Tetratheca*
Shrubs with numerous stems and pink or purple, pendulous flowers. Thirty-nine species are known with 21 found in the south-west.

***T. nuda*** has a fetid scent and grows in the Jarrah forest from Perth to Jurien Bay.

## The Milkwort Family — Polygalaceae

Mainly herbs or shrubs. There are 750 species known, with representatives in most countries of the world. The Sweet Pea Shrub, *Polygala myrtifolia*, from South Africa is often grown in gardens.

### *Comesperma*
A group of 40 species confined to the Australian region. Eighteen species are found in the south-west, and one in the Kimberley. Like the milkworts, some have variable flower colours — white, pink or blue.

***C. virgatum*** prefers swampy ground, and may be found from Perth to Bunbury.

***C. volubile*** is a twining species more widely distributed in the south-west.

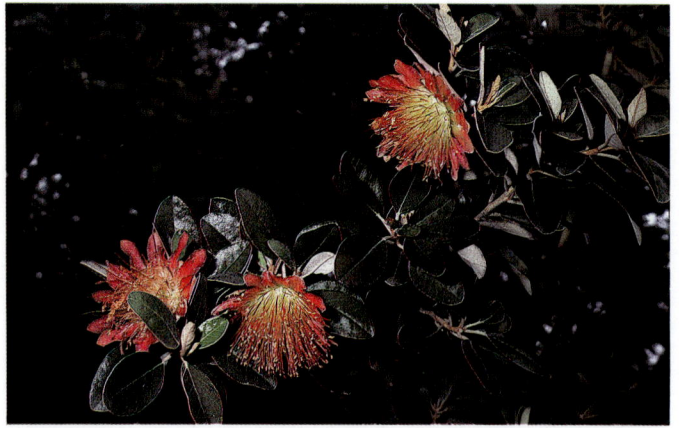

*Dodonaea hackettiana* (Jul.-Oct.) *(ABOVE)*
*Diplolaena dampieri* (Jul.-Sep.) *(LEFT)*

## The Dodonaea Family — Sapindaceae

Mainly trees or shrubs with most of the 1500 species concentrated near the tropical regions of the world.

### Dodonaea

Mainly shrubs with all except one restricted to Australia. They have inconspicuous flowers, but are usually covered in fruits, many with wings. There are 68 species of which 30 occur in Western Australia. They may be found growing anywhere from the Kimberley to the south coast.

**D. hackettiana** has colourful wings to its fruit and is restricted to the Perth region.

## The Cape Lilac Family — Meliaceae

A largely tropical family of mainly trees and shrubs. A total of 550 species are known.

**Cape Lilac,** or **White Cedar,** *Melia azedarach,* is widely cultivated as an ornamental tree. Its natural range includes the Kimberley district, also Iran, Afghanistan, Pakistan and Indonesia.

**Native Walnut,** *Owenia reticulata,* is a dense broad-leaved small tree which grows in the Kimberley and extends into parts of the Pilbara.

## The Citrus Family — Rutaceae

Nearly all these plants are aromatic shrubs or small woody perennials, and often have strongly scented flowers. There are about 1500 species mainly concentrated in the Southern Hemisphere, especially South Africa and Australia. In Western Australia the family includes the attractive, white-flowered *Crowea*, much used by florists, and *Chorilaena* from the Karri forest.

### Boronia

These are usually strongly-scented plants with conspicuous flowers. There are about 70 species in Australia, with 46 occurring in Western Australia.

**Scented Boronia,** *B. megastigma,* has brown flowers and is picked for its scent. It may be found growing in swamps near Albany.

**B. viminea** has many bright pink flowers and is widespread in the south-west.

### Diplolaena

Broad-leaved undershrubs with pendant, usually orange-coloured flowers. There are six species, all of which are confined to the south-west.

**D. dampieri** is a coastal species found from near Perth to Bunbury and on Rottnest and Garden Islands.

### Eriostemon

Mainly shrubs or small trees, with all 30 species restricted to Australia. There are 19 species in Western Australia.

**Pepper and Salt,** *E. spicatus,* has mauve flowers and is one of the first flowering plants to be noticed in spring. It occurs from near Geraldton to Augusta and inland to near Kalgoorlie.

## The Caltrop Family — Zygophyllaceae

A small family of herbs or shrubs mainly restricted to saline or arid environments. There are about 250 species altogether, mainly found in tropical regions of the world.

### Tribulus

These prostrate plants have spiny burrs like the introduced doublegee, which are dispersed by sticking in animals' feet. There are 20 species known, of which 11 are found in the north-west.

**Caltrop,** *T. hystrix,* grows in the Pilbara Region.

## The Geranium Family — Geraniaceae

The family is comprised of 700 mainly herb-like plants distributed over both temperate and tropical regions of the world. It includes the geraniums and pelargoniums, which are well-known garden plants.

### Pelargonium

These include the larger members of the family. They are strong-smelling, leafy, low shrubs. Most of the 250 species known are concentrated in South Africa. Four species are present in Western Australia.

**Rose Pelargonium,** *P. capitatum,* is widely naturalised near the coast. It originates from South Africa.

**Native Pelargonium,** *P. littorale,* occurs near the coast from Kalbarri to Cape Arid.

# The Carrot Family — Apiaceae (Umbelliferae)

A widespread family of herbs, which includes many economic plants (carrots, parsley, celery, angelica, fennel etc.). There are about 3000 species altogether.

## *Actinotus*

Mainly hairy herbs found in Australia and New Zealand. Six species are found in Western Australia.

**Flannel Flower, *A. leucocephalus*,** prefers rocky places from near Perth to Geraldton.

## *Eryngium*

Mainly spiny plants with bluish flowers. Some are grown in gardens, such as Sea Holly, *E. maritimum*, from the European-Mediterranean region. Two species grow in Western Australia.

*E. rostratum* is common from Geraldton to Albany, also in other parts of Australia and South America.

## *Trachymene*

Usually these plants have flowers in a dense head. There are about 40 species extending into Indonesia, with 18 in Western Australia.

**Rottnest Daisy, *T. coerulea*,** is a tall, carrot-like plant with white or blue flowers. It is found in coastal areas, mainly in the Perth area and on Rottnest Island.

## *Xanthosia*

Some of these plants have attractive flowers. All 15 species are restricted to Australia, and 11 occur in Western Australia.

**Southern Cross, *X. rotundifolia*,** has its flowers arranged in the form of a cross and grows in the Stirling Range and near Albany.

# The Periwinkle Family — Apocynaceae

This family is made up of about 2000 species, including the Periwinkle, *Vinca major*, which is often grown in gardens. It is not well represented in Australia.

## *Alyxia*

The genus includes about 80 species, which grow in Madagascar and Indonesia. Two are present in Western Australia.

*Anthocercis viscosa* (any month) (RIGHT)
*Ipomoea pes-caprae* (BELOW)

**Box-leaved Alyxia, *A. buxifolia*,** is a common, dark bush, which grows on dunes from Kalbarri to the Esperance area. It has white, tubular flowers and orange berries.

# The Tomato Family — Solanaceae

A widespread family of mainly herbs and shrubs with characteristic flowers and fruit in a berry. Economic species include potatoes, aubergines, tobacco and tomatoes. Many are poisonous, with toxic alkaloids, such as Deadly Nightshade, *Atropa belladonna*, and Thornapple, *Datura stramonium*. Black Nightshade, *Solanum nigrum*, is a common weed often erroneously called deadly nightshade by West Australians. There are about 2800 species, which are mainly distributed in South America, Africa and Australia.

## *Anthocercis*

These are generally tall shrubs with conspicuous white or yellow flowers. They all contain toxic alkaloids. Nine species occur in Australia, eight of which are found in Western Australia.

**Sticky Tailflower, *A. viscosa*,** has large fragrant flowers. It grows on the coast from Albany to Israelite Bay.

## *Solanum*

This is the most important branch of the family. They have many growth forms, ranging from herbs to trees, and include twining species as well. There are 1500 species distributed over most parts of the world. The 54 species in Western Australia include introduced species such as the Apple of Sodom, *S. sodomeum*, and Kangaroo Apple, *S. laciniatum*.

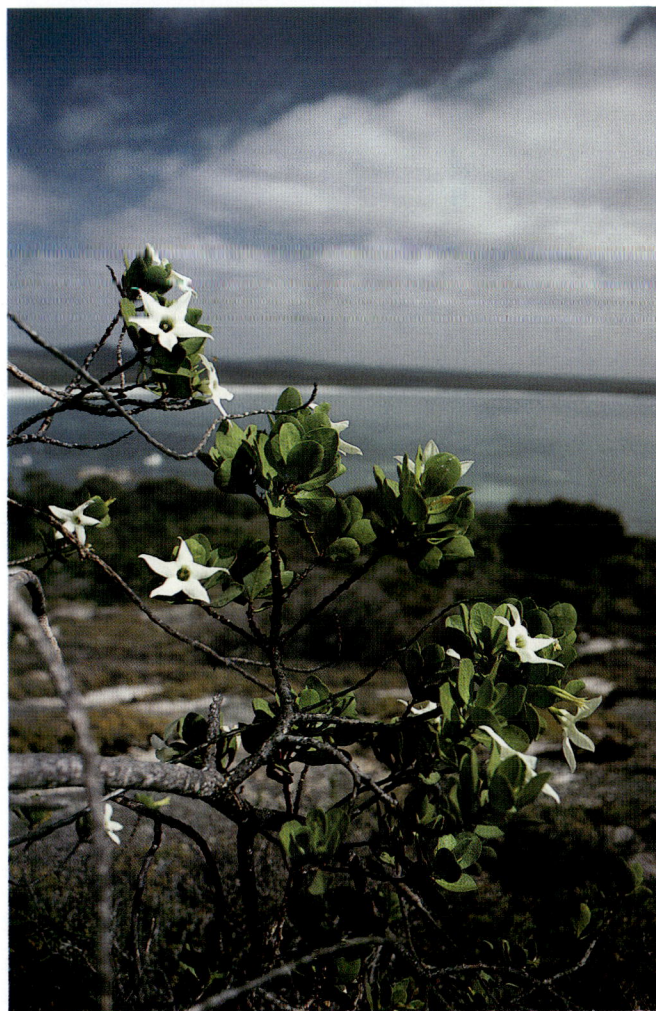

**Flannel Bush, *S. lasiophyllum,*** is a grey, woolly bush which is common in dry inland areas.

# The Morning Glory Family — Convolvulaceae

Usually these are twining or prostrate herbs with characteristic trumpet-like flowers. They include popular garden plants such as convolvulus and morning glory, *Ipomoea*, and also the Sweet Potato, *I. batatas*. It is a cosmopolitan family with over 1500 species. The parasitic plant dodder was once included in this family.

## *Ipomoea*
About 23 species are known from Western Australia, with most occurring in the north.

**Beach Morning Glory, *I. pes-caprae,*** is a common species found along tropical coasts around the world. It has long trailing stems straggling over sand dunes, and can be found as far south as Carnarvon.

# The Bogbean Family — Menyanthaceae

This is a small family of about 35 species found in temperate and tropical regions. It was once included in the Gentian family.

## *Villarsia*
Aquatic or semi-aquatic herbs in south-east Asia and Australia, some having floating leaves like waterlilies. Nine species occur in Western Australia. Many species have very restricted distributions because their habitats tend to be very isolated in this mainly dry country. Some are rare and endangered.

**Kingcup-Leaved Villarsia, *V. calthifolia,*** has bright yellow flowers and is only found in wet situations high on the Porongurup Range.

# The Lantana Family — Verbenaceae

This family includes a range of growth-forms — trees, herbs, lianas and mangroves. There are about 3000 species, which are found mainly in tropical and subtropical areas.

## *Avicennia*
Includes 16 species of mangrove with only one occurring in Western Australia. These trees are now normally put in a separate family — Avicenniaceae.

**White Mangrove, *Avicennia marina,*** is a widespread tree occurring in mangrove swamps around the world. It is common in the north, and there is also a small population growing at Bunbury in the south-west.

## *Cyanostegia*
Shrubs with spikes of bright blue or mauve papery flowers.

**Tinselflower, *C. lanceolata,*** grows on sandy or gravelly soils between Jurien Bay and Lake Grace.

# The Mint Family — Lamiaceae

Members of this family are mainly herbs and shrubs, but include some trees. They characteristically have quadrangular stems. The family is cosmopolitan and has about 3200 species. Well-known examples include many aromatic herbs such as peppermint, thyme, basil and marjoram.

## *Hemiandra*
A group of rigid shrubs with sharp-pointed leaves and two-lipped flowers. All eight species known are restricted to Western Australia.

**Snakebush, *H. pungens,*** has sharp-pointed leaves and pink flowers. It forms a useful groundcover plant in gardens, although it also has a variety with an erect growth-form. It ranges from Kalbarri to Albany.

## *Westringia*
A genus of shrubs endemic to Australia, where there are 26 species, five of which occur in the West.

**W. dampieri,** is mainly a coastal species with white flowers, and is often grown in gardens. It grows all along the southern coast and north to Kalbarri.

# The Foxglove Family — Scrophulariaceae

This is a large, cosmopolitan family of plants which are mainly herbs. There are 190 genera and 4000 species. Some well-known genera include *Veronica*, *Mimulus* and *Euphrasia*, all of which have native representatives in Australia; others include the mulleins, *Verbascum*, which have been introduced here. Altogether, the family is represented in Western Australia by about 45 species.

## *Peplidium*
A small genus of about eight species found only in Australia. They are creeping plants, which grow over rocks or on mud.

**P. muelleri** grows where ephemeral water may collect. It is widely distributed in the more arid parts of Australia, and includes several subspecies. Other species inhabiting wet mud include Mudmat, *Glossostigma drummondii*, which produces massed minute purple flowers.

# The Poverty Bush Family — Myoporaceae

A small family mainly concentrated in Australia, but extending into Asia, New Zealand and the Pacific. It is also represented in the West Indies. About 200 species are known, including some which are grown in gardens, such as Boobialla, *Myoporum floribundum*, from New South Wales. They are known as poverty bushes because they grow on some of the poorest pastoral land.

## *Eremophila*
These are mainly oily shrubs or small trees with red, orange, cream or mauve flowers, which grow mainly in the inland areas of Australia. 170 species are known with 125 in Western Australia.

**Pinyuru, *E. cuneifolia,*** has masses of purple flowers and is widespread from near the north-west coast to the desert fringe.

# The Bladderwort Family — Lentibulariaceae

This family is well-known for its carnivorous habits. The plants grow bladders on their roots, which are efficient suction traps designed to catch small aquatic animals. The European Bladderwort is a floating plant which has no roots and gains nutrients by catching waterfleas. Most Australian species grow on wet mud and have attractive flowers.

## *Utricularia*
This is a widespread group of 250 species, which includes the

**Peplidium muelleri**

European Bladderwort. There are 26 species known in Western Australia.

**Pink Petticoats, *U. multifida*,** grows in winter-wet depressions and near wet rocks. It produces masses of pink flowers in spring.

***U. inaequalis*** has large purple flowers and grows near Perth and Esperance.

# The Lobelia Family — Lobeliaceae

This is sometimes included as a subfamily of the bellflowers, Campanulaceae (only a few bellflowers occur in Western Australia in the genus *Wahlenbergia*). Lobelias are annual or perennial herbs and are often grown as garden plants. They grow mainly in temperate regions of the world, and there are about 1100 species known.

## *Isotoma*
Annual herbs with long stalked flowers or flower spikes.

**Woodbridge Poison, *I. hypocrateriformis*,** is an erect succulent plant with pinkish flowers. The plant continues flowering long after the roots die. It is widespread in the south-west from Kalbarri to Esperance.

**The Rock Isotome, *I. petraea*,** has white flowers and grows on rocky outcrops inland to central Australia. There are considerable genetic differences between isolated populations.

## *Lobelia*
A more widespread genus of about 400 species. Ten are known from Western Australia.

**L. gibbosa** is a summer-flowering species, flowering from November to March. It occurs in most of the inland south-west and in other parts of Australia.

# The Triggerplant Family — Stylidiaceae

The family is well known for its modified flowers which have a mobile column that strikes insect pollinators. The family is mainly restricted to Australia with about 155 species known. A few are also found in Indonesia, New Zealand, and the southern tip of South America. There are 140 species in Western Australia.

## *Stylidium*
This genus is mainly found in the south-west, with 130 of the 145 species known occurring in Western Australia. They are usually ephemeral herbs with creeping or erect stems.

**Boomerang Triggerplant, *S. breviscapum*,** has boomerang-shaped petals. It is widespread in the south-west.

**Pink Fountain Triggerplant, *S. brunonianum*,** has tall spikes of pink flowers. It extends from Kalbarri to the Stirling Range.

**Book Triggerplant, *S. calcaratum*,** is a small annual plant, which flowers on bare ground between shrubs. It is found between Kalbarri and Esperance.

**Climbing Triggerplant, *S. scandens*,** has recurved ends

to its leaves, and clings onto vegetation. It is found in the far south-west and the Stirling Range.

# The Fanflower Family — Goodeniaceae

This is a small family of mainly Australian species, although it extends as far as Japan and the Indo-Pacific area. Most are herbs with attractive blue, red, yellow or white fan-shaped flowers. Some grow into shrubs. In all there are about 300 species known.

## *Dampiera*
Mainly blue-flowered perennial herbs or shrubs. They are confined to Australia, with 70 species known in Western Australia.

**Woolly-headed Dampiera, *D. eriocephala,*** has dense woolly heads of flowers. It is found in the south-west from near Geraldton to the Stirling Range.

## *Goodenia*
Yellow, blue or white flowered herbs or shrubs, sometimes occurring in great numbers in semi-arid areas. Of the 170 species known, 106 occur in Western Australia.

**Blue Goodenia, *G. caerulea,*** flowers in late spring and is found throughout the south-west.

## *Lechenaultia*
This genus includes some very attractive species often grown in gardens. They have red, yellow, white or blue flowers. Only three of the 24 species known do not occur in Western Australia.

**Blue Lechenaultia, *L. biloba,*** commonly grows along roadsides in the south-west.

**Red Lechenaultia, *L. formosa,*** grows on sandy soils from north of Perth to the south coast, especially in the Stirling Range and Barrens area.

## *Scaevola*
Herbs or shrubs with some species being found throughout the tropical regions of the world. There are 90 species known of which 58 are found in Western Australia.

*Stylidium breviscapum* (Sep.-Dec.) *(BELOW)*
*Lechenaultia biloba* (Jul.-Nov.) *(RIGHT)*

**Royal Robe, *S. calyptera,*** is a large-flowered plant, which grows in the Jarrah forest.

# The Daisy Family — Compositae

These plants have large numbers of flowers concentrated into flowerheads, often with the outside flowers or sometimes the bracts being petal-like. This is one of the two largest plant families, with over 20,000 species known. There are many native species in Australia, especially everlasting daisies, also many have become naturalised including weeds such as Capeweed, *Arctotheca calendula*, Skeleton Weed, *Chondrilla juncea*, and Dandelions, *Taraxacum officinale*.

## *Brachyscome*
Daisy-like herbs, including 90 species mostly from the Australian region, with 19 found in Western Australia.

**Swan River Daisy, *B. iberidifolia,*** is widely cultivated for its attractive blue flowers. There is also a white-flowered form. It is found from Carnarvon to the south coast.

**Climbing Daisy, *B. latisquamea,*** is the largest species and climbs through bushes. It can be found from Shark Bay to Exmouth.

## *Cephalipterum*

*C. drummondii* is the only species. It is one of the everlasting daisies which carpets the countryside in many inland areas from Carnarvon to near Kalgoorlie. Mostly they are white but in some areas are a sulphurous yellow.

## *Cotula*
These daisies are prostrate annual herbs, with most of the 80 species known growing in South Africa.

**Waterbuttons, *C. coronopifolia,*** is one of the eight species which grow in Western Australia. It has yellow, button-like flowerheads and is widespread in all temperate regions of the world. It grows in wet pastures and along creek banks.

## *Craspedia*
These plants are tall with large, yellow, rayless flowerheads. Twelve species are recognized in Australia and New Zealand, but the genus needs revision.

*Scaevola calyptera* (Sep.-Nov.) *(ABOVE)*
*Brachyscome iberidifolia* (Aug.-May) *(TOP)*
*Brachyscome latisquamea* (Jul.-Sep.) *(RIGHT)*

**Billybuttons, *Craspedia* sp.,** is the only species found in Western Australia. It is common from Jurien Bay to Esperance.

## *Helichrysum*

A widespread group of 500 species, ranging through Europe, Asia and South Africa. In all, 26 species are known in Western Australia, including some which are everlasting daisies.

**Bushy Everlasting, *H. bracteatum*,** has both white and yellow forms. It is a tall plant which grows in the Jarrah forest and coastal plain near Perth.

**Rose-pink Everlasting, *H. davenportii*,** is an attractive pink species which grows in the Wheatbelt and from Kalgoorlie across to the Northern Territory.

## *Helipterum*

Some of the most spectacular everlastings found in Africa and Australia are included in this genus. About one hundred species are known with 45 occurring in Western Australia.

**Pink Sunray, *H. manglesii*,** occurs in woodland areas from Kalbarri to the Stirling Range and inland to near Kalgoorlie.

**Showy Sunray, *H. splendidum*,** has white flowers and occurs especially in areas of mulga from near Carnarvon to Kalgoorlie and inland towards the South Australian border.

## Olearia

Mainly shrubs with over 100 species in Australia and surrounding islands. Twenty-seven are known in Western Australia, some of which have attractive flowers.

**Coastal Daisybush, *O. axillaris,*** is a silvery bush which grows along the coast near Carnarvon and all around the south to New South Wales. It has scented foliage but insignificant flowers.

***O. paucidentata*** is a small, trailing bush with rather chrysanthemum-like flowers. It grows mainly in the Jarrah forest, and flowers during the summer.

## Podolepis

This is an Australian genus of only 20 species, ten of which grow in Western Australia.

***P. lessonii*** is a delicate plant with many yellow flowerheads on long narrow stalks. It is widespread from Kalbarri to Esperance.

## Podotheca

Another genus which is endemic to Western Australia. Only about five species are known.

***P. chrysantha*** is a sturdy, branching annual with larger yellow flowerheads than *Podolepis*. It ranges from near Jurien Bay to

*Helichrysum bracteatum* (Oct.-Dec.) *(BELOW)*
*Podolepis lessonii* (Aug.-Dec.) *(RIGHT)*
*Everlasting daisies (July - Sep.)* *(OPPOSITE)*

Augusta and inland to Kalgoorlie.

**Golden Long-heads, *P. gnaphalioides,*** has elongated flowerheads and grows on various soils, especially sand and clay from Kalbarri to near the Stirling Range.

## Senecio

This is the largest genus of flowering plants, with a worldwide distribution and over 2000 species. It includes many kinds of groundsel and ragwort. There are 17 species in Western Australia.

**Variable Groundsel, *S. lautus,*** has showy yellow flowers and is widely distributed from the Hamersley Range to the south coast.

## Waitzia

This is another group of everlasting daisies. All seven species are restricted to Australia.

**Golden Waitzia, *W. aurea,*** is widespread in the south-west.

**Fragrant Waitzia, *W. suaveolens,*** is an erect annual plant which grows up to 300 mm tall. It has white flowers with a yellow centre, and ranges from Kalbarri to the Fitzgerald River.

# The Vallisneria Family — Hydrocharitaceae

This is a group of fresh- or saline-water plants which grow partially or wholly submerged. About 100 species are known.

*Senecio lautus* (Aug.-Apr.) *(ABOVE)*
*Waitzia suaveolens* (Sep.-Dec.) *(RIGHT)*

## *Ottelia*

This is mainly a group of tropical plants, with only one species occurring in Western Australia.

**Swamp Lily, *O. ovalifolia*,** has broad floating leaves and attractive three-petalled white flowers. It grows in the Kimberley area and in the south-west from the Perth area to Israelite Bay.

## *Vallisneria*

Only about five species of this extraordinary plant are known, occurring mainly in tropical areas, especially in Australia. Two species are known from Western Australia. They are plants with strap like leaves which employ a unique method of pollination. They have tiny male flowers which break free and float to the surface of the water. Here they open out, holding the stamens above the water, where they can brush against female flowers. The female flowers merely touch the water surface, and their stems coil after pollination to return the developing seeds to the bottom.

**Ribbon Weed, *V. spiralis*,** is native to most of Australia, also Africa, Asia and parts of Europe. It grows naturally in the north-west, but is thought to have been introduced to the south-west, where it grows near Perth and in Lake Dumbleyung.

## The Seagrass Family — Posidoniaceae

This family has only one genus, and is found along southern Australian coasts and in the Mediterranean. It is sometimes included in the Zosteraceae, and both families are regarded by some plant taxonomists as belonging to the Pondweed family, Potamogetonaceae.

### *Posidonia*

These plants grow where they are not normally exposed at low tide, forming dense, grass-like beds. Nine species are known, one of which occurs in the Mediterranean.

**Fibreball Weed, *P. australis*,** occurs around southern coasts from Carnarvon to New South Wales. Its dead leaves often form banks at high tide mark, and the leaf fibres are frequently rolled by the waves into 5 cm balls.

## The Yam Family — Dioscoreaceae

Usually climbing plants with tuber-like roots, but sometimes herbs or shrubs. About 600 species are known, mainly growing in tropical regions.

### *Dioscorea*

These are slender plants which produce climbing stems up to two metres tall. They die back each year to a tuber at the base. There are about 600 species known, three occurring in Western Australia.

Warrine, **D. *hastifolia*,** has male and female plants — the females producing a winged, fleshy fruit. The tubers were eaten by local Aborigines. It is found from Perth to as far north as Shark Bay.

# The Grass Tree Family — Dasypogonaceae

This is one of the two grass tree families; the other is Xanthorrhoeaceae. Dasypogonaceae embraces about 63 species and is restricted to Australia, New Guinea and New Caledonia. The family includes *Acanthocarpus*, a prickly bush covering a large part of Rottnest Island; *Kingia*, a grass tree with knob-like flowerheads; and *Dasypogon*, which has similar flowers, but the plants are more slender. Other genera include *Lomandra*, which consist of lily-like plants.

## *Calectasia*
These plants are densely-leaved shrubs with blue, tinsel-like flowers. Two species are known, both restricted to southern Australia.

**Blue Tinsel Lily, *C. cyanea*,** grows near the coast from Jurien Bay around the south coast to Victoria.

# The Grass Tree Family — Xanthorrhoeaceae

This family forms one of the most characteristic features of the Australian vegetation. The plants have woody trunks topped by a head of grass-like leaves near the growing point. The leaf bases are packed together and cemented by a red gum, forming a thick, fire-resistant sheath around the trunk. Fires burn the free ends of the leaves to expose a charred trunk. The family is restricted to Australia and only one genus is recognized in the family.

## *Xanthorrhoea*
Thirty species are known, with eight occurring in Western Australia. Some do not have an above-ground trunk, but they all have tall spikes of flowers on a long stem.

**Black Grass Tree, *X. preissii*,** is the most widespread species in the south-west. It is variable, with some having their dead leaves strongly reflexed against the stem. This variety has in the past been regarded as a separate species.

*X. thorntonii* occurs in arid parts of Western Australia including the Little Sandy Desert.

# The Lily Family — Liliaceae

This is a large family which has recently been divided into many different families. Strictly speaking, there are no representatives of the lily family in Western Australia. However, the old broad classification is adhered to here for simplicity, although Dasypogonaceae and Xanthorrhoeaceae have been treated separately. The new families are indicated in brackets.

## *Borya* (Anthericaceae)
These plants have densely clustered, sharp-pointed leaves. There are ten species known in Australia, with seven in Western Australia, mostly in the south-west, but one in the Kimberley region.

**Pincushions, *B. sphaerocephala*,** grows on granite rocks from Kalbarri to the Fitzgerald River on the south coast. The plants dry out in summer, but become green again after rain.

## *Burchardia* (Colchicaceae)
These lilies have tall stems with umbels of flowers. Five species are known, all of which grow in the south-west.

**Milkmaids, *B. umbellata*,** flowers in early spring, especially in recently burned forest. It is also found in eastern Australia and Tasmania.

## *Chamaescilla* (Anthericaceae)
Only three species are known, all of which occur in Western Australia.

**Blue Squill, *C. corymbosa*,** usually has clear blue flowers, but also pale blue and white. It flowers August-September, occurring from near Perth to Esperance and extending across the south of Australia to New South Wales.

## *Dianella* (Phormiaceae)
A widespread genus of about 20 species occurring as far as Africa to the west and Hawaii to the east. Three species occur in Western Australia.

*D. divaricata* is a widespread species found in both arid and damp conditions from Carnarvon and Kalgoorlie to the Nullarbor Plain. The plants have rush-like leaves and tall flowerheads with scattered, mauve, tomato-like flowers. It has bright blue berries which are eaten by birds.

## *Johnsonia* (Anthericaceae)
These plants are unusual, rush-like lilies, with pink flowers which resemble hops. Only four species are known, all from the south-west.

**Native Hop, *J. lupulina*,** grows mainly on sandy or gravelly soils from south of Perth to Albany and the Stirling Range.

## *Sowerbaea* (Anthericaceae)
These are tufted plants with several leek-like flowerheads growing from the base. Five species are known, two of which grow in the south-west.

**Purple Tassels, *S. laxiflora*,** flowers from August to October and ranges from Kalbarri to near Albany on the south coast. There is also an isolated population near Exmouth.

## *Stypandra* (Phormiaceae)
An Australian genus which has only six species. Only one species is now recognized in Western Australia — it is so variable that in the past it has been regarded as two or three separate species.

**Blindgrass, *S. glauca*,** has leafy stems up to a metre tall with many blue or white, tomato-like flowers. It extends from Geraldton to Esperance, and is also found in eastern Australia and New Caledonia.

## *Thysanotus* (Anthericaceae)
The fringed lilies have unmistakable flowers with fringed petals, usually purple and arranged in umbels. Some have white or blue petals and others do not have flowers in an umbel. There are 47 species known, all of which grow in Australia. One ranges further afield into China. Forty-three occur in Western Australia.

*T. multiflorus* has a dense growth of basal leaves, and 200 mm stems with umbels of large flowers. Like most fringed lilies the flowers mainly open in the morning only. It is found from north of Perth to the Fitzgerald River.

**Twining Fringed Lily, *T. patersonii*,** has climbing stems which trail over vegetation up to about a metre tall. It is widespread in the south-west and occurs in other parts of Australia. *T. manglesianus*, formerly a subspecies, is now regarded as a separate species. It has anthers opening by terminal pores instead of slits.

## *Wurmbea* (Colchicaceae)
These plants usually have six-petalled pink or white flowers. There are 30 species in Australia and Africa, with 15 in Western Australia.

**Eight Nancy, *W. tenella*,** is atypical in that it usually has eight petals. It occurs in inland areas from Meekatharra to the Nullarbor Plain.

***Burchardia umbellata*** (Aug.-Sep.) *(TOP LEFT)*
***Sowerbaea laxiflora*** (Aug.-Oct.) *(TOP RIGHT)*
***Wurmbea densiflora*** *(ABOVE LEFT)*
***Thysanotus multiflorus*** (Sep.-Jan.) *(ABOVE)*
***Kingia*** (Jul.-Aug.) *(OPPOSITE)*

***W. densiflora*** has dense flower spikes and also grows in inland areas from the Murchison River to Leonora.

## The Iris Family — Iridaceae

This family includes many plants which have become naturalised in Western Australia, most of these garden escapees originating in South Africa. New genera which have become established include:

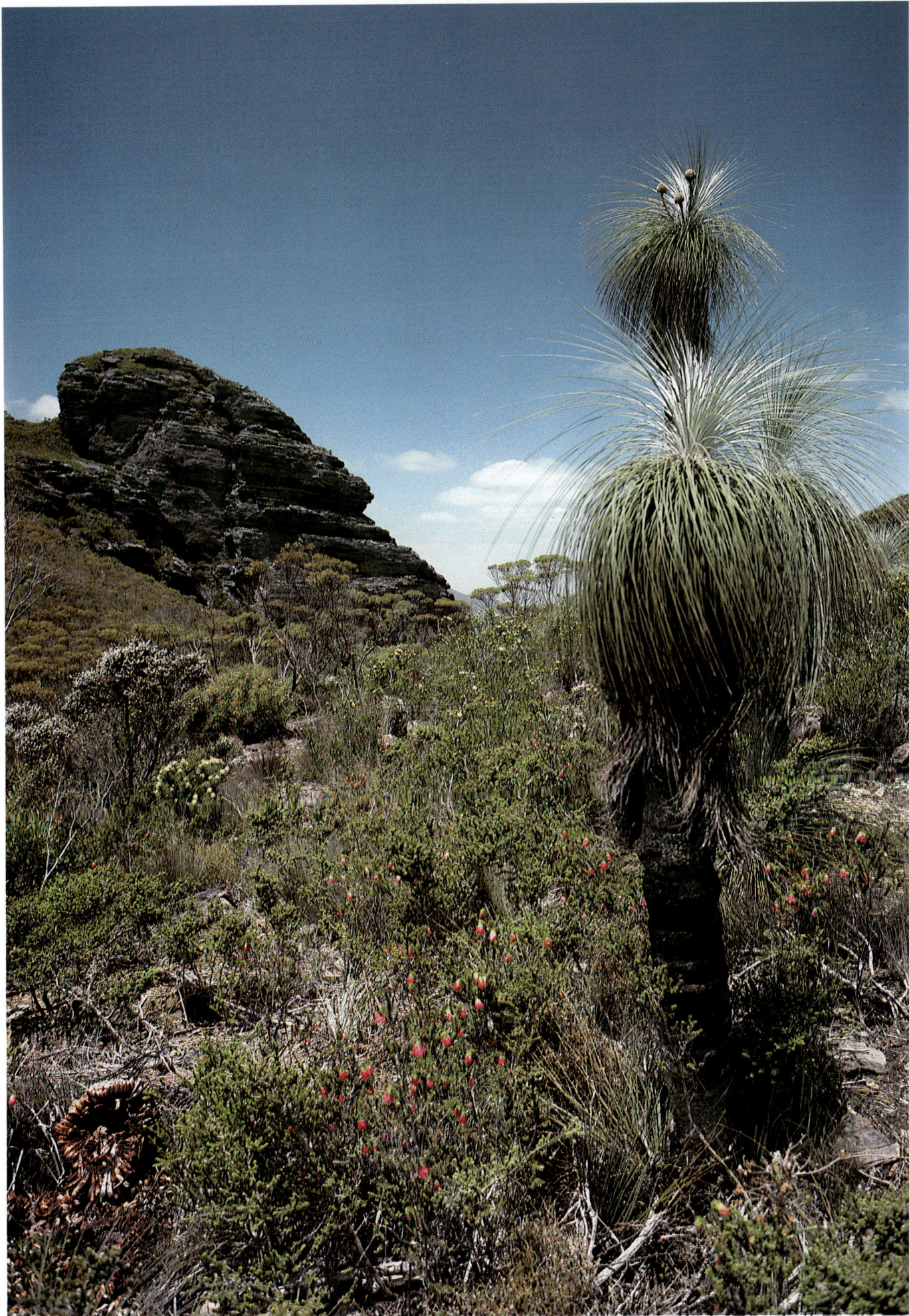

*Gladiolus, Watsonia, Babiana, Hesperantha, Freesia, Romulea, Homeria, Sparaxis* and *Ixia*.

## Orthrosanthus

This small group of seven irises is only found in Australia and America. All of the four Australian species occur in the south-west.

**Morning Iris, *O. laxus*,** has large, blue flowers and occurs from Geraldton to east of Albany.

## Patersonia

These irises have characteristic large, three-petalled flowers. There are 17 species known in Australia and some occur in New Guinea and Borneo. Western Australia has thirteen species, mainly with violet flowers, although *P. xanthina* has yellow flowers.

**Purple Flag, *P. occidentalis*,** is a common species which flowers September-December and occurs from Kalbarri to Esperance.

# The Orchid Family — Orchidaceae

This is a very diverse and often attractive group of plants which includes many with very strange-looking flowers that employ unique methods of pollination. The plants have minute seeds which can only germinate successfully in the presence of suitable fungi. The fungi allow the plants to grow in mineral-deficient places, such as in leached sand or as epiphytes on rainforest trees. About 17,000 species are known. A large num-

ber are known from Western Australia, and more new species are being described as the family becomes better known. Some local genera have rather insignificant flowers, especially the mignonette orchids, *Microtus* (8 species), and the leek orchids, *Prasophyllum* (18 species).

## Caladenia

This is a diverse group of about 85 species from Australia and nearby areas. About 68 are known in Western Australia.

**Cowslip Orchid, *C. flava*,** is a bright yellow species widespread from Kalbarri to Israelite Bay. The individual flowers vary greatly and some are strongly marked with red.

**Blue China Orchid, *C. gemmata*,** has large blue flowers, although there is a yellow variant. It is also found throughout the south-west.

**King Spider Orchid, *C. huegelii*,** is one of the many spider orchids, which have long trailing ends to the petals. It grows mainly in winter-wet depressions from south of Jurien Bay to Albany.

## Diuris

Flowers in this genus are known as donkey orchids because of their large, ear-like petals. At least 26 species are known, which are almost restricted to Australia (one occurs in Timor). The number of species present in Western Australia is at present unknown.

*Caladenia flava* (Aug.-Oct.)

There are at least six named species, but many varieties are also present which may deserve the rank of species.

**Common Donkey Orchid, *D. longifolia,*** is a widespread species occurring from Kalbarri to Israelite Bay and across to eastern Australia. It is made up of probably three separate species including *D. magnifica* from the south-west.

### *Elythranthera*
Only two species are known in this genus, both are restricted to the south-west.

**Pink Enamel Orchid, *E. emarginata,*** has large, shiny, pink flowers and occurs from north of Perth to Esperance.

### *Calaena*
An unusual flower with two species known currently. The flowers have a mobile part which is attractive to male thynnid wasps, the appendage mimicking the female wasp. The wasp is catapulted into the flower against the pollinia when the mechanism is tripped. Many other south-western orchids use wasps in similar ways, including the dragon orchids, *Drakaea*, elbow orchids, *Spiculaea*, and some spider orchids, *Caladenia*. Slipper orchids, *Cryptostylis*, use male ichneumons.

**Flying Duck Orchid, *C. nigrita,*** is widespread on sandy flats from Kalbarri to Esperance.

*Caladenia gemmata* (Aug.-Oct.) *(BELOW)*
*Elythranthera emarginata* (Sep-Nov.) *(RIGHT)*

### *Pterostylis*
These orchids are mainly made up of a group of winter-flowering species which are pollinated by small flies or midges. The flowers are greenish in colour and have odd shapes, with a mobile flap that temporarily traps insects inside the flower. About 100 species are known from Australia and New Zealand, with 20 occurring in Western Australia.

**Bird Orchid, *P. barbata,*** grows in woodland and winter-wet places from north of Perth to Albany. In profile the flower is bird-shaped and it has two long, lateral projections.

### *Thelymitra*
These orchids are known as sun orchids because their flowers only come out in the sun. There are over 50 species known, extending as far as the Philippines, and including 20 species in Western Australia.

**Lemon Orchid, *T. antennifera,*** has spikes of bright yellow flowers, and it grows on granite outcrops and in winter-wet depressions from Kalbarri to the south coast. Its range also extends as far as Victoria.

**Blue Lady Orchid, *T. crinita,*** is an attractive species with large, bright blue flowers. It mainly grows on lateritic soils from near Perth to Esperance.

## The Kangaroo Paw Family — Haemodoraceae

This family was once included in the Amaryllidaceae, known for

*Thelymitra crinita* (Sep.-Nov.) *(ABOVE)*
*Anigozanthos humilis* (Aug.-Oct.) *(RIGHT)*

garden bulbs such as *Amaryllis* from South Africa. It is now regarded as a separate family. The family name comes from the genus *Haemodorum*, which are tall plants, often with black, knot-like flowers and blood-red bulbs.

## *Anigozanthos*

The kangaroo paws are confined to Western Australia, with 11 species known. Their distinctive flowers are adapted for pollination by birds. The similar Black Kangaroo Paw, *Macropidia fuliginosa*, is put into a different genus.

**Mangles Kangaroo Paw, *A. manglesii*,** is named after Ellen Mangles, who was the wife of the first governor of Western Australia. It is the state floral emblem of Western Australia. It flowers prolifically in Kings Park and ranges from Shark Bay to near Busselton.

**Catspaw, *A. humilis*,** has short stems and orange flowers. It grows mainly on sand on the coastal plain from Kalbarri to east of Albany.

## *Conostylis*

These plants are closely allied to the kangaroo paws and are also only found in the south-west. There are about 30 species, mainly with tight clusters of yellow or white flowers.

**Red Bugles, *C. canescens*,** is an unusual variant with reddish flowers, which is sometimes put in a separate genus. It grows mainly on sand from Jurien Bay to Perth.

**Bristly Cottonheads, *C. setigera*,** is a more typical representative and is widespread from north of Perth to Albany.

## *Tribonanthes*

These plants have hairy, felt-like, white flowers, which come out early in the season. They mainly grow in wet areas and on granite slopes.

***T. longipetala*** grows near swamps and on shallow soils on rocks, from north of Perth to the Stirling Range.

## The Reedmace Family — Typhaceae

These reeds, characterised by their club-like seedheads, are often known as bulrushes. There are about ten species in the world altogether, with two in Western Australia.

## *Typha*

This is the only genus in the family.

**Bulrush, *T. domingensis*,** grows in winter-wet depressions and along swamp margins in the south-west and north of Western Australia. It is also widespread in warmer parts of the world. It has narrow, erect, green leaves. Another species, *T. orientalis*, has been introduced into the south-west. This has a thicker seedhead, and broader, glaucous leaves, with more pendulous tips. It is native to eastern Australia.

## The Sedge Family — Cyperaceae

There are about 4000 species of sedge. Many occur in Western Australia, especially in the following genera: *Cyperus* (46 spp.), *Lepidosperma* (30 spp.) and *Schoenus* (60 spp.). There are only six species of *Carex* native in Western Australia.

## *Baumea*

These reeds have tall, cylindrical, leaf-like stems. The genus has in the past been included in *Cladium*, a genus familiar to people from Europe.

**Jointed Twig-rush, *B. articulata*,** grows in waterlogged soil, often covering shallow lakebeds, where it produces peat. It grows in the Kimberley and in most of the wetter south-west as far east as the Fitzgerald River.

## The Southern Rush Family — Restionaceae

These plants are restricted to the Southern Hemisphere, being mainly found in South Africa and Australia. There are several genera, with about 300 species known, many of which are confined to the south-west.

## *Restio*

A genus with about 25 species mostly confined to Western Australia, although the genus is still in the process of revision. They are known as cord rushes and generally have a dense matted growth-form.

## The Grass Family — Poaceae

One of the largest plant families, with over 8000 species known. There are many native species in Western Australia, and also many which have been introduced, some as forage plants, others as weeds. Of the better-known grasses, there are six native species of bent grasses (*Agrostis*), one Brome Grass (*Bromus*), two meadow

*Anigozanthos manglesii* (Sep.-Nov.) *(ABOVE)*
*Typha domingensis* *(RIGHT)*

grasses (*Glyceria*), and seven species of *Poa*. The introduced veldt grasses (*Ehrharta*) from South Africa are major weeds in bushland areas in the south-west. Marram grass, *Ammophila*, has also been introduced to help stabilize sand dunes.

## Spinifex
These grasses of the genus *Spinifex* are not the tussock grasses typical of the arid interior, which belong to the genera *Triodia* and *Plectrachne*.

**Long-leaved Spinifex, S. longifolius,** grows on coastal sand dunes and sandy bays from Albany northwards. It is also present in Indonesia.

## Stipa
There are about 300 species of spear grasses in the world, and 34 of these are native to Western Australia.

**Feather Speargrass, S. elegantissima,** grows through bushes, which support its tall flower spikes. The diffuse seedheads have a silky look from a coating of fine hairs. When

mature, the heads break off and are dispersed by the wind. The plant occurs from Shark Bay to Esperance and across Australia to New South Wales.

## Triodia
These grasses, together with the genus *Plectrachne*, grow into the hummocks which are typical of the arid interior of Australia. They mainly grow on sandy or stony ground, in places which are not subject to inundation, even after exceptional rainfall. The grasses grow mainly in the regions which experience summer rain, or very erratic rainfall, as opposed to the dry, winter-rain areas which usually have mulga or mallee vegetation. The plants may grow into tall spiny tussocks up to six metres in diameter. Often the centre of old tussocks dies out, leaving a ring of living grass. The grass thrives on infrequent fires, which are now mainly started by lightning. In the past the desert areas were managed by Aborigines, who burned spinifex on a regular basis. This fire regime maintained the grass in optimum condition for native mammals, many of which are now extinct or on the verge of extinction. There are altogether about 35 species of *Triodea* and about 11 of *Plectrachne*.

**Lobed Spinifex, T. basedowii,** is one of the common species on sandplains and dunes.

# FAUNA

The animal kingdom includes everything from mammals and birds to insects, worms and microscopic protozoa. Western Australia includes a vast array of very interesting animals, including examples from most of the world's main faunal groups.

## Origins and Diversity

Australia's animals have two main origins. Some species or groups have evolved in Australia since it was part of the great southern continent Gondwanaland, over 100 million years ago. This part of the fauna has links with species in other parts of Gondwanaland, especially South America, with which it shares a marsupial fauna and a wide variety of insect groups. There are also links with southern Africa, similar to those found in the flora. The other main origin involves species which have entered Australia since the land mass approached South-east Asia. These were able to make the crossing mostly during the ice ages, when sea levels were low enough for animals to island-hop, or walk into Australia. This is how rodents came and many tropical butterflies. The remaining fauna came over millions of years by freak accidents, or, for the more mobile species such as birds, by active migration.

Since arriving in Australia, all species have been subject to the process of evolution, which in the course of time leads to change and increased diversity. The rodents clearly illustrate this process, with probably only one species of mouse coming to Australia about 15 million years ago, and some rats about one million years ago. These animals have evolved into the 60 species of native rodent found in Australia, which comprise over a quarter of the mammalian fauna.

The same process of evolution has led to the great diversity of less mobile species, especially the insects which are associated with plants. Each species of plant has a range of insects which are entirely dependent upon it — the numbers range from a few unique species associated with each small herb, to several hundred for each major tree species. The inevitable consequence is that insect diversity is many times that found in any flora.

Another great change brought about by the ice ages was the arrival of hominids in the form of some of the early ancestors of the Aborigines. It seems likely that they came at least 100,000 years ago. This brought about an enormous change in the fauna, with the extinction of the last of the great marsupials and giant flightless birds. It also facilitated the arrival of other species of fauna, such as the Bushfly, which could not have survived in Australia without the presence of mankind. The evolving Aborigines introduced the dingo at least 3500 years ago, which probably resulted in the mainland extinction of both the Tasmanian Devil and Tasmanian Wolf — the last major marsupial predators (they persisted in Tasmania, where there were no dingoes).

## Adaptation to Arid Environments

As Australia moved north after it broke with Antarctica, the climate changed from temperate rainforest, with rivers and lakes all over the continent, to one of increasing aridity and temperature extremes. The climatic change meant that places which once had flamingo-shimmering swamps, progressively dried out and were replaced by sizzling deserts. Those animals which could adapt survived, but many others became extinct. This was the fate of Australia's flamingoes.

Adaptation to arid conditions takes time; in the early stages it may only be a matter of behaviour, learning how to detect small quantities of fresh water and changing activity times to reduce water loss. Long-adapted species may also have acquired changes in their anatomy and physiology which improve their ability to live in arid areas. They may be able to radiate heat efficiently or have kidneys which can retain more body water. This time factor is illustrated by the rodents: the mouse which came in 15 million years ago has evolved into many desert-dwelling species, while none of the rats which came in during the last million years has become adapted to arid areas.

The marsupial fauna has all been present in Australia since the arid conditions began, so many species are well adapted to living in desert areas. For these animals it is a mistake to apply our set of values and regard the desert as a hard place to live in; as long as they stick to the rules of the environment — as the Aborigines did — life can be as easy as anywhere else. For these animals, cold and wet conditions are probably much harder to cope with than hot and dry, and desert species may find it more difficult to survive in the wet, south-west corner of the country than in their normal habitat. That is perhaps why some of the species which were abundant and widespread at the time of European settlement, first died out in the south-west, near the extremities of their range. One example may be the Bilby, which was last seen in Mosman Park near Perth in 1928, yet still persists in the arid Western Desert.

## Breeding Seasons

In areas with a predictable climate the breeding seasons are usually geared to coincide with annual rainfall — many birds in the south-west use the spring flush of insects to feed their young. On the other hand northern species often make use of the summer wet in the Kimberley region.

In arid regions one of the adaptations is to not have a regular breeding season — breeding there is opportunistic and may be set in motion by rain, whenever it may fall. Kangaroos and wallabies have another interesting strategy — they have a young joey in the pouch or developing all the time, so that when rain does fall the joey already has a head start and can grow rapidly. If no rain comes, the joey dies before it becomes a drain on its mother, and within a

**Feral horses can be found in most places, especially in the north. Horse Reserves were set aside early in the century to provide horses for the Army.**

few weeks is replaced by another.

It is interesting that kangaroos employ a mechanism of delayed embryonic development which allows embryos to wait until the pouch is vacated. This system shortens the time it takes to replace a joey in the pouch — so they are ready should rain fall — and it allows females to produce young long after their last mating, even when no males are around.

## Interrelationships

In the natural environment there is a complex network of interdependence between species. On the gross level animals breathe out the major component that plants need for growth — carbon dioxide. In return plants release into the atmosphere oxygen which animals require for respiration. There was no oxygen in the atmosphere before plants began the process of photosynthesis and life had to depend on other means of respiration. As we get to know more about natural ecology we find that every species fits into the system, like the parts which make up a grand building. Some may be pillars, others part of the intricate detail of priceless stonemasonry. If some are lost the building collapses, the loss of others may only reduce its appeal.

An example may be seen with rat kangaroos, which used to be one of the most abundant marsupial groups, living across Australia like rabbits. The Boodie (Burrowing Bettong) lived in the northern part and the Woylie (Brush-tailed Bettong) in the southern areas. The Boodie is now extinct on the mainland and the Woylie only lives in a few reserves in the south-west. In one area where it was studied it was found that it needed fire to regenerate its habitat, but fire also temporarily removed most of its food. However, truffle-like fungi emit a scent to attract Woylies after a fire. This allows the Woylies to survive until other foods become available, while in return the fungi have their spores dispersed. The fungi are also an essential component of a healthy forest, because they form a mycorrhizal association with the trees, bringing minerals to their roots. Loss of the Woylie may lead to the loss of the fungi, decline in the trees and the spread of disease and insect attack. Perhaps this is one of many factors involved in the decline of Australian forests.

Another interrelationship exists between farming and the loss of rare banksias due to the decline in Black Cockatoos (as well as through land clearance). It has been found that farming turns bushland country into an appealing habitat for desert-loving Galahs. The Galahs are aggressive birds and take over nest holes which were normally used by Black Cockatoos. The result has been that the cockatoos have now largely disappeared from the Wheatbelt area. The effect on banksias has been that they no longer have anything which can kill the caterpillars that eat the seeds in banksia cones, because the cockatoos are the only birds with strong enough beaks to break open infected cones. The loss of the cockatoos has resulted in all the banksia seeds being eaten by caterpillars.

Natural ecosystems are built on complex interrelationships such as these. Normally the web is resilient in the face of change — when one species is absent another takes on more of its role (hopefully a parasitic wasp will kill the caterpillars); or the loss of a subset, such as the rare banksia-caterpillar-cockatoo, has no great impact on the whole. However, we all need to be aware that, although changes are slow and often imperceptible on our timescale, our impact on the Australian environment has already severed untold numbers of these links. Many of our desert marsupials are already extinct, and we have to sadly admit that there is little doubt that these extinctions merely represent a more visible manifestation of what we can expect, as larger numbers of species fall out of Australia's tattered web of life.

## Introduced Species

Since people first came to Australia they have brought with them species which were not native to the country. Human parasitic worms and insects are likely to have been the first invaders, like the Bushfly. It is surprising that no domesticated animals or plants were adopted by the Aborigines until the Dingo came at least 3500 years ago. This lack has been more than made up for during the 200 years of European settlement. Mammals are the most visible additions to the fauna, with domestic stock all over the continent. Sheep and cattle can be seen in most places. They are managed in the pastoral areas of the Eremaean Province, where they live in semi-feral conditions. Goats have also become pests in the pastoral areas, in places building up into large numbers.

The lack of any native large grazing or browsing mammals and the absence of any lion-sized predator has left the arid areas of Western Australia open to colonization by exotic species. The one-time beasts of burden, the Camel, Donkey and Horse, have all invaded these areas. Attempts are now being made to contain their numbers, particularly horses in the Pilbara region and donkeys in the Kimberley. Australian camels are now being exported to the Middle East where they are used as racing animals, because tough, wild camels no longer exist there. Camels and their Afghan drivers were first brought to Australia in the 1840s as a means of outback transport, but when roads and railways were built, the drivers were sent home and their camels shot or liberated.

Rabbits were brought here in very early days, because most seafarers kept rabbits and often liberated them on islands to provide food on later visits. The rabbit population on Carnac Island, now cleared, may have dated from this activity. Mainland Australia proved difficult to colonize with rabbits, because domestic rabbits were soon killed by local predators. This changed when a consignment of wild rabbits from England was brought into New South Wales in 1858. In the next 60 years the species spread across the southern part of the continent. Attempts were made to prevent it reaching farming areas in Western Australia, by building the Rabbit-proof Fences. This may have been the largest such undertaking in the world, since the Great Wall of China. The first fence stretched for 1824 kilometres through remote arid parts of the country, from near Esperance to the north coast near Broome. Good rainfall in the Nullarbor led to huge populations of rabbits, which completely swamped the fence as the region returned to its usual aridity, and the rabbits moved west. Rabbits may now be found everywhere except in the Kimberley Region, while the fence has become a wildlife hazard, particularly for migrating emus.

Foxes were originally brought in for foxhunting, but rapidly spread with the growing rabbit population. They came into the south-west in the 1930s and are thought to be largely responsible for the sudden demise of many marsupial species. Other introduced feral mammals include the Cat, Black Rat, House Mouse,

**Rabbits may be seen anywhere except in the Kimberley.** *(BELOW)*
**Numbats were on the verge of extinction until fox control brought about a dramatic turnaround in their population. This warning notice is at Boyagin Rock Reserve where Numbats have been successfully reintroduced.** *(RIGHT)*

Pig and Palm Squirrel (only in Perth). Hares have not become established here, nor some other species which were liberated, such as Indian Blackbuck and various species of deer. The growth of deer farming could change this.

The mammals only represent a small proportion of the exotic animals in the fauna. Some birds have become established, including two doves, White Swans (at Northam) and some birds from other parts of Australia, such as the Kookaburra, Rainbow Lorikeet and Chestnut-breasted Finch. The only other introduced vertebrates are species of fish, which include the Rainbow Trout, Mosquito Fish and Carp.

Invertebrates form the bulk of introduced species. Many are pests of crops such as the House Fly, Mediterranean Fruit-Fly, Blow Fly (causing fly-strike in sheep), and large numbers of species of greenfly, such as the Lucerne Aphid. The Garden Snail, Potato-Root Eelworm and Lawn Beetle are also present. Introduced Earthworms are common and useful additives to farmland, where native worms are lacking. The Liver Fluke is not found here, largely because there were no suitable snail hosts (the snails have now become established in the Perth area). Some insects are now being liberated in biological control programmes, such as African dungbeetles for the control of Bushflies. They have been used because cow dung is now the main breeding habitat used by Bushflies (in earlier days they were dependent upon human and dog excrement). The dung also reduces productivity, because it smothers pasture vegetation in the absence of insects that can disperse it. Many species of beetle are required, because each has a different breeding cycle and climate preference and no one species can disperse dung in all parts of Western Australia at all times of year.

POISON RISK AREA
FOX BAITS OF DRIED MEAT OR EGGS CONTAINING 1080 POISON HAVE BEEN LAID ON THIS RESERVE.
• 1080 IS POISONOUS TO HUMANS AND DOMESTIC ANIMALS
DANGER

# Conservation

The most valuable form of conservation is to preserve large areas of habitat, in as natural a state as possible. This will conserve the majority of species living in the area. Management is of prime importance, particularly in regard to fire, because a mosaic of burning was a prime factor in preserving natural vegetation, producing habitats made up of areas in various stages of regeneration. In the Wheatbelt sufficiently large reserves do not exist, so no management can bring back species, such as some jewel beetles, which may already have gone forever.

The conservation of particular species at risk becomes a separate issue, where preservation of habitat is not enough. The Numbat, for instance, used to be widespread across Australia, but recently declined to small populations in a few reserves. There is little doubt it would have become extinct without intervention. Research demonstrated that the Fox was the main culprit, and fox poisoning has resulted in dramatic increases in Numbat numbers. The same conclusion was reached concerning Rock Wallabies, and they are increasing again now that a programme of Fox control has been introduced. Green Turtle eggs are being protected by Fox control near Exmouth, and it may be possible to re-establish Boodies in the Shark Bay area after Fox and Cat control — they only survive on some offshore islands in the absence of these predators. Spinifex burning management and Fox control may also save the Bilby in the Western Desert, while elaborate fences are being used to keep Foxes out of the few remaining habitats occupied by the Western Swamp Turtle.

**Parts of the Rabbit-proof Fence are still maintained to prevent animals entering the farmed area from the pastoral country. Migrating emus met the fence in 1976 and about 80,000 died.**

# *Mammals*

THE MAMMALS found in Western Australia include a single, egg-laying species (the Echidna) and a wide range of pouched animals (marsupials). The remaining mammals are placentals — those with young that develop in a womb. These include many bats, rodents, and a wide range of marine mammals, including seals, whales and the Dugong.

## The Egg-laying Mammals — Monotremata

This group of mammals appears to have been a primitive branch of the main evolutionary tree. Few fossils have been found to indicate their evolutionary history, but they are known to have occurred in South America. The three living species are restricted to Australia and New Guinea — the Platypus is restricted to eastern Australia and the Long-Beaked Echidna to New Guinea.

**Short-beaked Echidna,** *Tachyglossus aculeatus,* occurs throughout Australia. Its spiny armour and ant-eating habits seem to have made it able to avoid competition and predators, and utilize all habitats. In hot regions they are mostly active at night, while in cool times of year they may be out in the middle of the day. The female lays a single, soft-shelled egg directly into a pouch. The young echidna hatches in about 10 days, and drinks milk exuded from pores on the mother's mammary glands. It leaves the pouch after three months, but does not

**Common Dunnart**

become independent until about a year old.

## The Pouched Mammals — Marsupialia

The main feature of this group is that the young are born when they are still at an early embryonic stage, with only their front limbs well developed. They follow a saliva trail licked by the mother, which guides them into the pouch, where they attach themselves onto a teat. Some species have pouches facing forwards, like the kangaroos, others including bandicoots have it opening towards the rear, while Numbats have no pouch at all, and have their young exposed. The marsupials have a more widespread distribution than monotremes, there being many species in South America, and one, the Opossum, extending into North America. They also occur naturally in New Guinea and some adjacent islands. Feral populations exist in New Zealand and England.

## The Predatory Marsupials — Dasyuromorpha

This group includes the Thylacine and Tasmanian Devil, both of which occurred in Western Australia until a few thousand years ago. The Western Quoll is the largest species in Western Australia. The remaining species are small, often mouse-sized animals, which usually feed on insects, centipedes, spiders and small vertebrates. There are 21 kinds in the West including the Mulgara, the Dibbler, antechinuses, phascogales, dunnarts,

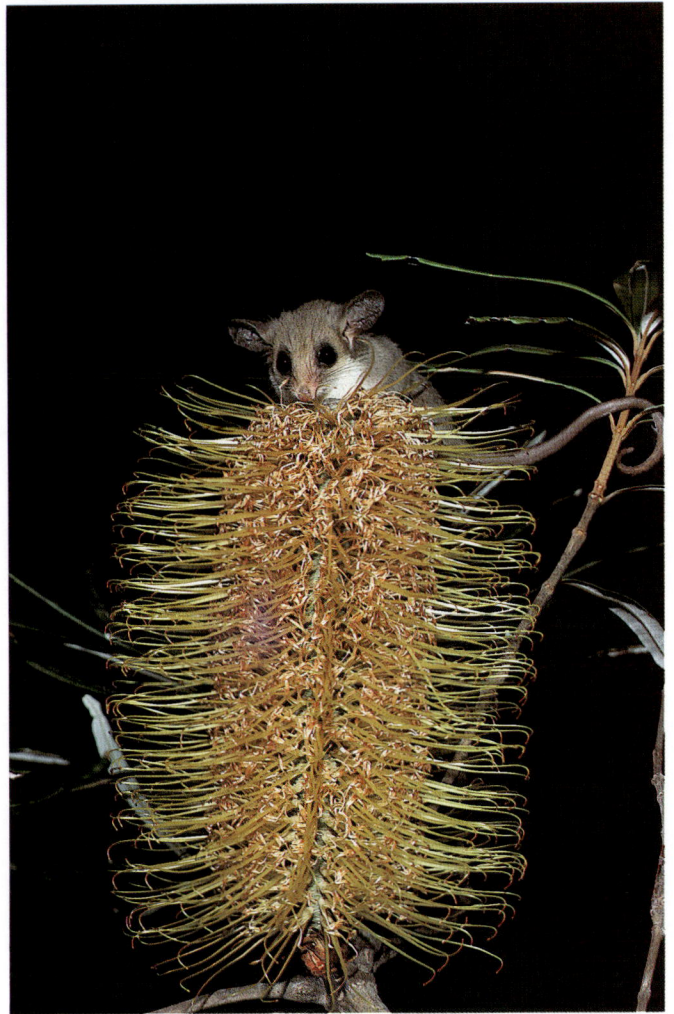

**Sugar Glider** (ABOVE)
**Pygmy Possum** (RIGHT)

planigales and the Ningaui.

**Western Quoll, *Dasyurus geoffroii,*** is a white-spotted animal with ferret-like characteristics. It used to occur all around Australia, but is now restricted to a few areas in the south-west.

**Northern Quoll, *D. hallucatus,*** is similar and occurs from the east Pilbara to Queensland.

**The Common Dunnart, *Sminthopsis murina,*** is a voracious little predator which lives in the south-west and also in south-east Australia and Queensland.

Two further animals appear to belong to this group although differing somewhat from the others.

**Numbat, *Myrmecobius fasciatus,*** is the marsupial version of an anteater. This is the faunal emblem of Western Australia. It is an attractive striped animal with a squirrel-like tail. They are active in daylight, because that is the time when termites are accessible to them. They used to occur across the south of Australia as far as New South Wales, but declined as the Fox increased in numbers. The decline was still occurring in the 1970s at Dryandra — one of their few remaining haunts in the south-west — and extinction seemed inevitable. It is encouraging to see that the trend has been reversed by excluding Foxes, and populations have increased sufficiently for liberations to be made at the nearby Boyagin Rock Reserve.

**Marsupial Mole, *Notoryctes typhlops,*** is a desert animal which mainly inhabits sand ridges from the area near Broome to Alice Springs and South Australia. Little is known about the animal because of its burrowing habit. They are blind with vestigial eyes and feed on a variety of insects.

## The Omnivorous Marsupials — Perameloidea

This group comprises the bandicoots and bilbies, which differ from the previous group by having the toes on the hind feet reduced, like those of the kangaroos. Most of the species have had their numbers greatly depleted since European settlement, with the Pig-footed Bandicoot and Lesser Bilby now extinct. They are mostly rabbit sized animals, with sharp noses for eating invertebrates from holes dug by the forepaws. The Southern Brown Bandicoot, *Isoodon obesulus*, is still quite common in the south-west, while the Golden Bandicoot, *I. auratus*, is common on Barrow Island and still present in the Kimberley district. The once abundant Western Barred Bandicoot, *Perameles bougainville*, is now only found on Bernier and Dorre Islands. The Bilby, *Macrotis lagotis*, as mentioned earlier, although once widespread, is now restricted to a few desert areas between Broome and Alice Springs.

## The Herbivorous Marsupials — Diprotodonta

This is another diverse group which is characterized by two lower front teeth projecting directly forwards. It includes all the possums, koalas and kangaroos; also the unique Honey-possum.

### Koalas and Wombats — *Vombatidae*
In earlier times the Koala inhabited Western Australia, but became extinct before the end of the last ice age. Fossil remains have been found at Devil's Lair near Margaret River. The only current representative is the Hairy-nosed Wombat, *Lasiorhinus latifrons*. This badger-sized animal lives in burrows between the Nullarbor and the coast near Eucla.

### Possums and Gliders — *Phalangeroidea*
This group, mostly adept tree-climbers, includes those animals

with adaptations similar to flying squirrels. Some can live away from trees in rocky areas.

**Sugar Glider, *Petaurus breviceps*,** is the only glider in Western Australia, where it is restricted to the Kimberley region.

**Brushtail Possum, *Trichosurus vulpecula*,** is common in the south-west. It often takes to living in the roofs of houses, waking people at night. Its characteristic scent, like rotting gum leaves, can be smelt in areas where it lives. A similar northern species occurs from Exmouth to north Queensland.

**Ringtail Possum, *Pseudocheirus peregrinus*** used to be common in the extreme south-west but numbers have declined recently. It has a longer prehensile tail.

**Pygmy Possum, *Cercartetus concinnus*** is a mouse-sized animal which is an important pollinator of some flowers, especially banksias. It is scarce but still found in scattered locations around the south-west.

**Honey-possum, *Tarsipes rostratus*,** is a unique, minute, long-nosed animal which feeds exclusively on nectar from banksias and other flowers such as bottlebrushes. Its natural range extends from Shark Bay to Eyre on the south coast. It prefers heath-like habitats where it has a reliable food source with some plants flowering every month of the year.

## The Kangaroo Family — *Macropodoidea*

These animals all have a bipedal, hopping mode of progression, and have strong hind legs. The larger kangaroos use a heavy tail to serve as a counterbalance, to conserve energy while hopping. Smaller members have a long, rat-like tail. The kangaroos remain plentiful, but most other species are seriously depleted or extinct in Western Australia. This has been the fate of the Long-nosed and Broad-faced Potoroos.

**Brush-tailed Bettong, *Bettongia penicillata*,** is a small species feeding mainly on insects, fungi and seeds. It used to occur all across southern Australia, but is now only found in a few small reserves in the south-west.

**Boodie, *B. lesueur*,** had an even more extensive range, and was extremely abundant on the mainland, but is now only found on Bernier, Dorre and Barrow Islands.

**Quokka** (BELOW)
**Brush Wallaby** (RIGHT)

**Spectacled Hare-wallaby, *Lagorchestes conspicillatus*,** is a small, short-nosed animal which still persists in tussock grasslands and shrubs in the Pilbara and more arid parts of the Kimberley. It is abundant on Barrow Island.

**Rufous Hare Wallaby, *L. hirsutus*,** was once common, but, like the Banded Hare-wallaby, is now only found on Bernier and Dorre Islands.

**Northern Nailtail Wallaby, *Onychogalea unguifera*,** is a larger, kangaroo-like animal which is common in the Kimberley and extends across to Queensland. The related Crescent Nailtail Wallaby used to occur in the south-west, but is now extinct.

**Brush-tailed Rock-wallaby, *Petrogale penicillata*,** used to be abundant on rocky outcrops from the extreme north-west to Esperance. The numbers have greatly declined through Fox predation, but they are increasing where Fox control is practised.

**Rothchild's Rock-wallaby, *P. rothschildi*,** is another species found in the Pilbara. The Short-eared Rock-wallaby, *P. brachyotis*, is also present in the Kimberley, together with the smaller Narbarlek, *Peradorcas concinna*.

**The Quokka, *Setonix brachyurus*,** is a small, short-nosed wallaby which is common on Rottnest Island. Its normal habitat is in dense vegetation bordering swamps, and local populations persist in suitable places throughout the south-west corner of Western Australia.

**Tammar Wallaby, *Macropus eugenii*,** prefers semi-open woodland areas in the south-west. Its numbers are greatly reduced on the mainland, but it is common on Garden Island near Perth.

**The Brush Wallaby, *M. irma*,** is a larger animal with a long, rope-like tail. It is a sedentary species and is locally common in the south-west, but has declined markedly in recent years and is in need of active conservation measures.

**Agile Wallaby, *M. agilis*,** is the most frequently seen wallaby in the north from Broome to Rockhampton in Queensland. The other common macropod in the region is the Antilopine Wallaroo, *M. antilopinus*, which is a larger animal.

**Western Grey Kangaroo, *M. fuliginosus*,** is a large species which is abundant across the southern part of Australia as far as New South Wales. They are not sedentary like the Brush Wallaby, but roam large areas and may collect into mobs

**Western Grey Kangaroo**

of over fifty animals. Their young are presumably too large to be killed by Foxes.

**Euro, or Hill Kangaroo, *M. robustus*,** prefers hilly country in the more arid parts of Australia. It is widespread and common everywhere except the south-west corner and northern Kimberley. It is similar to the Red Kangaroo but smaller and does not have white underparts.

**Red Kangaroo, *M. rufus*,** is the largest living marsupial, weighing up to 86 kg and standing over 2 metres tall. (It would have been completely dwarfed by the giant kangaroos which became extinct before the last ice age.) These animals prefer open plains, unlike the Euro, and are distinctly white below. They are common throughout the arid regions, increasing in numbers after good rains. Both the Red Kangaroo and Euro have red and grey colour varieties.

## The Placental Mammals — Eutheria

This group comprises all the other mammals: bats, cats, seals, whales, rabbits, rodents, deer, monkeys etc. They have in common the characteristic of having their young develop in a womb, attached to the mother by a placenta. This enables the young to be born at a relatively advanced stage of development.

### The Bats — *Chiroptera*

The bats evolved from early insectivorous mammals in tropical rainforests. With the power of flight they have been able to colonize even the most isolated islands, such as New Zealand, and over the years many have come into Australia from south-east Asia. About 60 species are known in Australia with 32 in Western Australia.

### Flying Foxes — *Pteropodidae*

These are generally large bats which feed on fruit and nectar. Unlike most other bats they have large, functional eyes. Many are highly social, living in dense colonies. They are mainly tropical and only three occur in the north-west: the Little Red Flying-fox, the Black Flying-fox and the Northern Blossom-bat. They are important pollinators of some flowers, especially gum trees and mangroves.

**Black Flying-fox, *Pteropus alecto*,** roosts in noisy colonies in the trees during the day, and flies long distances to flowering gums at night. There is a large colony at Millstream in the Pilbara, many others in the Kimberley. Very occasionally the bats are seen as far south as Perth.

## Normal Bats — *Microchiroptera*

These are mainly insectivorous bats which use echolocation instead of eyes to see by. This means of navigation provides a very detailed picture of the environment, in some respects providing more information than sight, especially with regard to distance and speed of movement. West Australian bats include representatives from many families. The false vampires are anomalous in having large eyes and being predators. The rest include horseshoe bats, sheathtail bats, mastiff bats, long-eared bats, bent-wing bats, wattled bats, broad-nosed bats, pipistrelles and species of *Eptesicus*.

## False Vampires — *Megadermatidae*

This is a small family of five species found in Africa, Asia and Australia. They are predatory bats with large eyes.

**Ghost Bat, *Macroderma gigas*,** is the largest species and is restricted to Australia where it is found from the Pilbara to Queensland. It used to be more widespread, and its range is continuing to contract. It is Australia's only predatory bat, catching frogs, lizards, birds and small mammals as well as insects. It swoops on its prey, enveloping it in its wings and killing with a powerful bite.

## Sheathtail Bats — *Emballonuridae*

These bats have a loose membrane around the tail, which allows greater movement in the hind legs, so that the animals can walk more easily than other bats. They are found in South America, Africa, south Asia and in the Australasian region.

**Common Sheathtail Bat, *Taphozous georgianus*,** is a common cave-dwelling species. It forages up to 8 km from the roost and normally has a slow, straight flight pattern. It is found mainly in the north, often in old mineshafts.

## The Rodents — *Rodentia*

These animals are characterised by gnawing front teeth which continue to grow throughout life, so that they never wear down. They are a very successful group, making up more than half of the known species of mammal. About 2000 have been described in the world. Twenty-nine species are native to Western Australia, but, like some of the smaller marsupials, they have been seriously affected by changes since European colonization. Many are now extinct or greatly reduced in numbers. These include Gould's Mouse, the Heath Rat, stick-nest rats, and three species of hopping-mouse.

## Aquatic Rats — *Hydromyini*

These are mainly found in New Guinea, but with two Australian species. They live in damp places and have water-repellent fur.

**Water-rat, *Hydromys chrysogaster*.** This is a large rat, often weighing over 1 kg. It lives by rivers and streams, or saline marshes. It has webbed feet and is well adapted to aquatic life, feeding on mussels, crayfish, frogs etc. In Western Australia it is found in the south-west, Pilbara coast and Kimberley. It has also been found at Dorre Island, where it lives on the sea shore. It is unrelated to the European Water-rat, which is a vole.

## Rabbit-rats etc. — *Conilurini*

This is a mainly Australian group where there are 40 species — another two occur in New Guinea. It includes most of our native rodents ranging from tree-rats, rock-rats and stick-nest rats to a wide range of mice.

**Pebble-mound Mouse, *Pseudomys chapmani*,** is an interesting little mouse, which lives in the Hamersley and Chichester Ranges. It is thought that the mice build mounds of pebbles around their holes to precipitate dew in this arid environment. Its unoccupied mounds show it had a wider range in the recent past.

**Spinifex Hopping-mouse, *Notomys alexis*.** This is a widespread species of the arid inland which extends to the north-west coast. It has long hind-legs used for hopping, and sleeps in deep burrows to avoid the heat of the day. Mouse populations fluctuate with rainfall, large numbers often appearing after good seasons.

## Newer Native Rats — *Murinae*

These are true rats which have entered Australia probably during the last million years. They belong to the same genus as the introduced Black and Brown Rats.

**Bush Rat, *Rattus fuscipes*,** lives in some of the more damp areas around the coast in the south-west and in eastern Australia. It is a small rat, weighing only up to about 200 g.

**Long-haired Rat, *R. villosissimus*,** and **Pale Field-rat, *R. tunneyi*,** live in the Kimberley and along the Pilbara coast. They sometimes appear in enormous numbers after widespread rain.

# Carnivorous Mammals — Carnivora

This group has teeth primarily designed for killing prey and eating flesh, but fruit and other vegetable foods are also eaten, for example by Foxes which will often eat blackberries. Seals, here described under marine mammals below, also belong to the carnivores.

**Dingo, *Canis familiaris*.** As a feral domestic mammal this is a very recent addition to the Australian fauna. It is closely allied to the domestic dogs found in South-east Asia and India, and is thought to have been brought into the country by Aborigines more than 3500 years ago. It is still widespread, particularly in the more remote parts of the country. They will at times form into packs like domestic dogs, and kill or mutilate flocks of sheep. This behaviour brings them into conflict with pastoralists and in many areas they are still systematically shot, trapped or poisoned.

# Marine Mammals — Cetacea, Sirenia and Pinnipedia

The marine environment has been invaded by several groups of mammal. The degree of adaptation depends on the length of time which has elapsed since they adopted this environment. Thus the Water-rat is only marginally different from ordinary rats, having water-repellent fur and webbed feet. Seals on the other hand have much more modified limbs, although their ancestors may have looked rather like Sea Otters. At the other end of the scale are the whales and dolphins, which became marine animals a very long time ago.

## Fur-seals and Sea-lions — *Otariidae*

These are the eared seals which appear to be slightly less adapted to the marine environment than the 'true' seals, because they still

**Spinifex Hopping-mouse**

retain traces of their terrestrial ancestry in the form of the ears and ability to use their hind feet for walking. Two species occur along the south-west coast — the Australian Sea-lion, *Neophoca cinerea*, which extends up to the Abrolhos Islands off Geraldton, and the New Zealand Fur-seal, *Arctocephalus forsteri*, which is only found on rocky shores and islands along the south coast. The former has a blunt snout and the latter a distinctly sharp one. The young are born late in the year, especially in November.

## Dugongs and Manatees — *Sirenia*
These are unusual marine mammals in that they are herbivores. They have a whale-like tail and no hind limbs. The Manatee lives in South America and feeds mainly in fresh water on aquatic weeds. It has been used to control Water Hyacinth, which blocks waterways in the Americas.

**Dugong, *Dugong dugon,*** is found in tropical waters in the Indo-Pacific region. It is a truly marine mammal, and feeds largely on sea grasses. In most parts of the Dugong's range numbers have greatly declined, but they remain relatively stable in Australian waters. They occur all along the northern coast from Shark Bay to Gladstone in Queensland. There is a relatively large population in the Shark Bay area.

## Whales and Dolphins — *Cetacea*
This is the most ancient group of marine mammals, and includes the Blue Whale, which is the largest animal ever to have lived on the planet. Whales and dolphins are commonly seen around West Australian coasts. Dolphins often come into harbours and estuaries including the Swan River at Perth. They can be trained to become accustomed to people, as has been done at Monkey Mia in Shark Bay and at Bunbury. About 36 species of Cetaceans have been recorded in Australian waters and the numbers of whales have increased since whaling ceased. Hump-back Whales regularly move north along the coast for the winter to have their young and return in October-November on their way back to Antarctic waters.

# *Birds*

HAVING THE POWER OF FLIGHT, birds have more frequently found their way to Australia than the relatively sedentary mammals. However, this is not true for the living large flightless birds, all of which are remnants of species surviving on parts of Gondwanaland — the Rhea in South America, Ostrich in Africa, Cassowary in Queensland and New Guinea, and the Emu in Australia. Others became extinct before European exploration, such as the Moa in New Zealand, some huge birds in Madagascar and the Megornithids in Australia, which had massive bills.

**Australian Pelican**

The bird fauna has many affinities with South-east Asia, although it is not easy to distinguish those groups which originated in Australia and spread to Asia from those which went in the other direction. Australian groups include the honeyeaters and magpies. (Common names such as 'magpie' are misleading, because they originate from superficial similarities with European birds — the Australian Magpie does not belong to the same family as the European and American Magpies.)

People visiting from the Northern Hemisphere may find a few familiar species, some of which are migrants. Species which migrate here from the Palaearctic region include swifts, and many

**Darter** *(RIGHT)*
**Emu** *(ABOVE*

waders such as turnstones and stints. Wagtails are also increasingly being seen in Australia. Other birds only migrate north in winter within Australia or into Indonesia, such as some cuckoos and the Rainbow Bee-eater.

## The Flightless Birds — Casuariiformes

**Emu, *Dromaius novaehollandiae*.** This is a large bird, standing up to about two metres tall. They are found throughout Western Australia, although restricted in populated areas. They live in the Karri forest as well as in the spinifex of the north. They are nomadic, moving towards the wetter south-west in times of severe drought. About 80,000 were shot or died in 1976 when drought brought migrating birds up against the State Barrier Fence (the up-graded Rabbit-proof Fence, which is still used to keep migrating animals and Emus out of the farmed area of the south-west).

## The Open Sea Birds — Spenisciformes and Procellariiformes

These include penguins, albatross, petrels and shearwaters. About six species of albatross, three prions and nine petrels occur around the coast; they are usually seen only after storms.

**Little Penguin, *Eudyptula minor*.** Several species of penguin are occasionally seen in Australian waters. This is the only resident species in the south-west. It is about 40 cm tall and breeds under dense bushes on offshore islands, such as Penguin Island near Rockingham. The birds remain close to the breeding grounds throughout the year.

**Wedge-tailed Shearwater, *Puffinus pacificus*,** breeds on islands on the west coast as far south as Carnac, off Fremantle. The birds come in at night to feed the chicks. Other species include the Fleshy-footed and Little Shearwaters. Shearwaters nest in holes and are often known as mutton-birds.

## The Grebes, Pelicans, Gannets and Cormorants — Podicipediformes and Pelecaniformes

Only one pelican occurs here and three gannets (including boobies). There are six cormorants, one darter, two tropicbirds, three frigatebirds and three grebes, including the Great Crested Grebe, which is also found in Africa and Europe.

**Australian Pelican, *Pelecanus conspicillatus*.** This is the largest pelican and occurs all over Australia. It opportunistically colonizes temporary freshwater lakes after heavy rain, especially Lake Eyre in South Australia. It does not dive like the Brown Pelican in America.

**Pied Cormorant, *Phalacrocorax varius*.** The larger of the pied species, this bird is mainly found in marine environments along the west and north coasts.

**Little Black Cormorant, *P. sulcirostris*,** prefers fresh water. It occurs throughout Western Australia apart from the arid centre.

**Darter, *Anhinga melanogaster*,** has a much longer, snake-like neck. The same species occurs in Africa.

## Herons and Egrets — Ciconiiformes

There are eleven herons and egrets, including a night heron, three bitterns, three ibises, two spoonbills and the Jabiru stork. The Brolga crane found in the north looks similar, but is more allied to rails than storks.

**Reef Heron, *Ardea sacra*,** is common around the coastline where it feeds on crabs and small fish. It has both a white and grey form.

**Great White Egret, *Ardea alba*.** This is a large, attractive bird which used to be killed for its plumes. It is found in all of the warmer parts of the world.

**Rufous Night Heron, *Nycticorax caledonicus*,** has a

**Pied Cormorant**

short neck and feeds mainly at night. It ranges over most of Western Australia.

**Jabiru, *Ephippiorhynchus asiaticus*,** is resident across northern parts of Australia and extends along the Pilbara coast.

**Sacred Ibis, *Threskiornis aethiopica*,** has a long curved bill. It occurs mainly in the Kimberley and eastern Australia, but is also present near Perth. The more widespread Straw-necked Ibis has glossy black wings.

## The Ducks and Geese — Anseriformes

West Australian species include the Magpie Goose in the Kimberley, the Cape Barren Goose in the Recherche Archipelago, the Black Swan and fourteen ducks.

**Black Swan, *Cygnus atratus*,** prefers permanent fresh or brackish swamps and lakes. It is most frequently seen in the south-west, but may be found wherever there is water. It is native to Australia, but has been introduced into New Zealand where it became a pest.

**Australian Shelduck, *Tadorna tadornoides*.** Most shelduck are adapted to saline waters. This duck prefers open water both fresh and saline, especially in the south-west. They nest in caves on Rottnest Island and are commonly seen on the sea shore and salt lakes.

**Black Duck, *Anas superciliosa*,** is the commonest duck species, and is found throughout Australia. It is allied to the Mallard and interbreeds with it.

## The Birds of Prey — Falconiformes

Western Australia possesses a rich array including seven kites, three goshawks, three eagles, two harriers, six falcons and the Osprey.

**Wedge-tailed Eagle, *Aquila audax*.** This is a large bird with a characteristic tapering tail. It ranges throughout Australia, but like many birds of prey, has been greatly reduced in farming areas where insecticides have been widely used. Carrion forms a large part of its diet, and it is often wrongly blamed for killing already dead lambs. Many are shot because of this habit. Birds sometimes collect around roadkills in outback areas like vultures in Africa. Black Kites are also often seen singly at roadkills.

**Osprey, *Pandion haliaetus*,** is found in all Australian coastal regions and similar areas in most parts of the world. It is smaller than the White-breasted Sea-eagle which also occurs around the coast. They both catch fish in their talons. The Osprey nests on rockstacks around the coast; several nests are present on Rottnest Island.

**Australian Kestrel, *Falco cenchroides*.** Similar to kestrels found in Europe. It can often be seen hovering over grasslands looking for insects or lizards. The Grey Falcon, *F. hypoleucus*, has a similar habit.

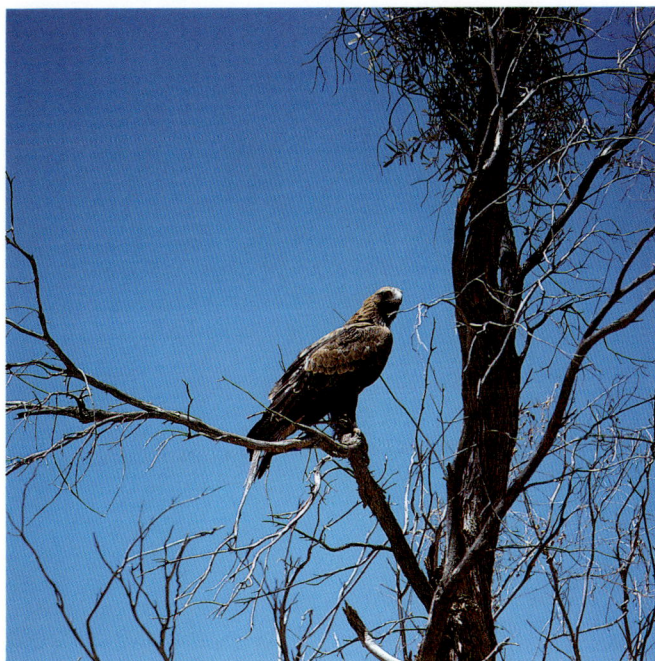

**Black Swan** (ABOVE)
**Wedge-tailed Eagle** (RIGHT)

# The Gamebirds and Quail — Galliformes and Gruiformes

These include the mound-builders, and six kinds of quail, nine rails and crakes (also the Brolga mentioned under herons), coots, swamphens and the Australian Bustard.

**Mallee Fowl, *Leipoa ocellata*,** used to be common all over the southern half of Western Australia, but is now greatly reduced, probably through Fox predation. Like other mound-builders this species incubates its eggs in warm mounds of soil. Some species use rotting vegetation or volcanic heat but the Mallee Fowl uses sand heated by the sun, carefully tended by the male bird. When the chicks hatch they are immediately independent and run off into the bush. The related Scrub Fowl occurs in the east Kimberley, and extends into Indonesia and Pacific islands.

**Australian Bustard, *Ardiotis kori*.** These birds are well adapted to the arid interior of Australia, making opportunistic use of areas receiving rainfall. They can be seen anywhere except in the wetter south-west corner, but like bustards everywhere, have been seriously depleted by shooting. They are relatively safe now that they are protected.

**Purple Swamphen, *Porphyrio porphyrio*,** is a large bluish bird with a red bill. It is found in the south-west and Kimberley, also in eastern Australia.

**Eurasian Coot, *Fulica atra*,** is common on city lakes in many parts of the world, and occurs throughout Australia. It is a black bird with a white splash on the head.

# The Waders and Gulls — Charadriiformes

Large numbers of waders occur in Western Australia, including many which come here for the northern winter. Enormous numbers arrive near Broome in the spring on their way south and return in the autumn. They include two oystercatchers, 13 dotterels, turnstones, snipe, whimberels, curlews, various sandpipers, tattlers, stints, the Sanderling, godwits, two stilts, avocets, stone curlews, three gulls and 12 terns.

**Pied Oystercatcher, *Haematopus ostralagus*.** A prominently black and white bird with red bill and legs. Also found in Europe, Asia and Africa. Occurs all along our coasts with the Sooty Oystercatcher, *H. fuliginosus*, which is only found in Australia. They feed on mussels and other shellfish.

**Banded Stilt, *Cladorhynchus leucocephalus*.** Has very long legs for wading. It congregates on the Rottnest Island salt-lakes during the summer, and returns to inland salt-lakes where it breeds after exceptional winter rains. Often seen in company with some Red-necked Avocet, *Recurvirostra novaehollandiae*, which have long, upward-curved bills.

**Southern Stone-curlew, *Burhinus magnirostris*,** is a tall brown bird which likes open plains, especially airfields and has a haunting, mournful call. It is found throughout Australia.

**Silver Gull, *Larus novaehollandiae*.** The common gull species. Other gulls include the large, black-backed Pacific Gull.

**Caspian Tern, *Sterna caspia*.** This is the largest tern with a black cap and red bill. Terns feed by hovering over water and diving for fish near the surface.

# The Pigeons and Doves — Columbiformes

There are 23 native species in Australia with 12 in Western Australia. In addition the Senegal Turtledove from Africa is well established in the south-west and also local populations of the larger Spotted Turtledove from India. The domestic Pigeon is also present in cities. The common species include some with crests, like the grey coloured Crested Pigeon and Red-plumed Pigeon from the Pilbara.

**Common Bronzewing, *Phaps chalcoptera*,** is found throughout Australia. It is a large bird which takes off with a characteristic clapping of wings. It likes eating seeds, including those from poison plants.

**Diamond Dove, *Geopelia cuneata*.** A small, ground-dwelling dove seen in grassy plains in the north. They may come in large numbers to water.

# Parrots and Cockatoos — Psittaciformes

This group is well represented in Australia with a total of about 53

**Purple Swamphen** (TOP LEFT)
**Pied Oystercatcher** (TOP RIGHT)
**Southern Stone Curlew** (LEFT)
**Galahs** (ABOVE)

species — 27 in Western Australia. They include the nectar-feeding lorikeets, large cockatoos, parrots, rosellas, the Cockatiel and the Budgerigar, also the rare Ground and Night Parrots.

**Rainbow Lorikeet, *Trichoglossus haematodus.*** This is a very noisy bird and one of the most brilliantly multi-coloured. It is native to the Kimberley region where it has a distinct red collar, differing from those in eastern Australia. It is also found in Indonesia, and has been introduced into Perth.

**Purple-crowned Lorikeet, *Glossopsitta porphyrocephala,*** is common in the south-west, especially in the Karri Forest.

**Long-billed Black Cockatoo, *Calyptorhynchus baudinii,*** is a large black bird which often flies in noisy flocks. It is

restricted to the south-west. There are two species, which are hard to tell apart. Another black species is the Red-tailed Cockatoo which is widespread in Australia.

**Galah,** or **Pink-and-grey Cockatoo, *Eolophus roseicapillus,*** prefers arid Australia where is can be a pest. It has extended its range into farmed areas and Perth. Other small cockatoos include Major Mitchell's, which is also pink.

**Little Corella, *Cacatua pastinator,*** is abundant in the north-west and Kimberley Regions.

**Port Lincoln Parrot, *Barnardius zonarius.*** This is the commonest green parrot, which is also known as the Twenty-eight, from its call. Others in the south-west include the Red-capped Parrot, and the Western Rosella, which appear

**Boobook Owl becomes an innocent victim of a barbed-wire fence. Kangaroos and Emus are more frequent casualties** *(RIGHT)*
**Spotted Nightjar** *(ABOVE)*

green in flight. In the inland and north-west the Mulga Parrot is a common green parrot.

**Rock Parrot,** *Neophema petrophila,* is a small green parrot seen around the coast and Rottnest Island.

**Budgerigar,** *Melopsittacus undulatus,* lives in arid Australia, where it feeds on grass seed. They breed well after good rains, and may occur in large numbers.

**Weiro, or Cockatiel,** *Nymphicus hollandicus,* is a small grey and white bird with a similar habit to the Budgerigar.

## The Cuckoos, Owls and Nightjars — Cuculiformes, Strigiformes and Caprimulgiformes

Cuckoos are well known for their habit of laying eggs in other bird's nests. All except the Pheasant Coucal have this parasitic habit in Western Australia. There are 11 species altogether; most are more or less migratory, many flying north into Indonesia for the winter. Their piercing calls herald the start of spring.

Five owls are found in Western Australia. They include the widespread Barn Owl, and the similar Masked Owl.

**Boobook Owl,** *Ninox novaeseelandiae,* is the usual species heard calling at night. The call is reminiscent of the European Cuckoo.

Nightjars are the other major nocturnal group of birds, and mainly feed on insects. Three species are present.

**Tawny Frogmouth,** *Podargus strigoides,* has a repetitive booming call, which is sometimes confused with that of the Boobook Owl.

**Spotted Nightjar,** *Eurostopodus argus,* may be encountered over most of the country. It rests on the ground, where it is well camouflaged.

## The Kingfishers and Bee-eaters — Coraciiformes

Kingfishers get their name from Europe where the only species

feeds on fish. Most Australian species prefer dry land and feed on lizards and insects. Common species include the Red-backed and Sacred Kingfishers.

**Kookaburra,** *Dacelo novaeguineae,* is not native to Western Australia, but has become well established in the south-west.

**Blue-winged Kookaburra,** *D. leachii,* is common in the north.

**Rainbow Bee-eater,** *Merops ornatus.* This attractive bird migrates south in the spring, and nests in holes dug in grassy slopes. It is adapted to catching insects on the wing, especially bees.

**Roller, or Dollar Bird,** *Eurystomus orientalis.* This is another blue bird, which can be seen in the north. Some very colourful species are familiar to people visiting Africa.

## The Swifts, Swallows and Martins — Apodiformes and Hirundinidae

Swifts are remarkable birds in that they are the only birds almost fully adapted to life in the air, flying day and night, only having to alight when nesting.

**Fork-tailed Swift,** *Apus pacificus.* The only swift present in Western Australia, it has the typical sharp curved wings of a swift, and may be seen flying high in the air anywhere. They do not alight in Australia at all, and nest in Japan and other parts of Asia.

Swallows and Martins are similarly adapted to life in the air, but settle at night and when resting. They belong to the Passerines and are not allied to the swifts.

**Welcome Swallow,** *Hirundo neoxena,* is similar in appearance to the Barn Swallow, *H. rustica,* the familiar species from other parts of the world. Welcome Swallows are resident in the south-west and Pilbara Region.

**Fairy Martin,** *Petrochelidon ariel,* are small, swallow-like birds common throughout the country. They usually live in groups around their nesting areas, in culverts and caves.

## Perching Birds — Passeriformes

The majority of the birds seen in bushland areas belong to this group, which, although very diverse, have a more recent common origin than the birds previously described. They include the swallows and martins above.

### The Pittas — Pittidae
Very brightly coloured birds of the rainforest floor. They are mostly migratory in Australia, but the Rainbow Pitta, *Pitta iris,* is sedentary in coastal areas of the Kimberley region.

### The Scrub-birds — Atrichornithidae
Rather small, drab birds confined to Australia. They are rarely seen, but, being related to Lyre Birds, have loud songs and mimic other species.

**Noisy Scrub-bird,** *Atrichornis clamosus,* used to be widespread in the south-west, but is now restricted to Two People Bay near Albany.

### The Pipits and Wagtails — Motacillidae
Small, ground birds including wagtails which wag their tails in the vertical plain, unlike the Willy Wagtail which wags horizontally. These wagtails are only vagrants to Australia.

**Richard's Pipit,** *Anthus novaeseelandiae.* A common pale-brown bird often seen walking along tracks in open country, or flying ahead of cars.

### The Magpie-larks — Grallinidae

**Magpie-lark,** *Grallina cyanoleuca.* A conspicuous black-and-white, ground-feeding bird, often seen on roads, where they can build dome-shaped mud-nests on poles or trees.

### The Cuckoo-shrikes — Campephagidae
A family related to minivets, although superficially looking somewhat like cuckoos and shrikes. Six species occur in Western Australia.

**Black-faced Cuckoo-shrike,** *Coracina novaehollandiae,* is a grey bird which shuffles its wings conspicuously on alighting.

### The Babblers — Timaliidae
This is a somewhat diverse group in Australia, including quail-thrushes, babblers, whip-birds, wedgebills and choughs. Eight species occur in Western Australia.

**White-browed Babbler,** *Pomatostomus supercilliosus,* is a noisy bird which quickly makes its presence known in the bush, often with cat-like noises. They are social, and build many conspicuous nests.

**Chiming Wedgebill,** *Psophodes occidentalis.* A small, crested bird whose call is characteristic of mulga and arid scrub areas. It incessantly sings *Did-you-get-drunk.*

Kookaburra *(TOP LEFT)*
Splendid Wren *(BOTTOM LEFT)*
Red Wattlebird *(TOP RIGHT)*
Double-bar Finch R.J. TAYLOR *(BOTTOM RIGHT)*

### The Australian Wrens — Maluridae
These include the brightly-coloured fairy wrens, emu wrens, grass wrens and bristlebirds. They are usually small birds, with long tails that are often held erect.

**Splendid Wren,** *Malurus splendens.* The dominant male has brilliant blue plumage, other males and females in territorial groups are pale grey-brown. It ranges from Shark Bay to the south coast. Eight other fairy wrens occur in the west, including the White-winged Wren, which prefers mulga and spinifex country, also the Red-backed Wren in the Kimberley region.

### The Warblers — Sylviidae and Acanthizidae
The former group are well known in the Old World, where they include the Willow Wren and Chiff-chaff. Here they are represented by reed warblers and songlarks. The Australian Warblers are represented in the west by 19 species of mainly small, brown birds. They include thornbills, weebills, whitefaces, scrub wrens and field wrens. The Western Warbler is well-known for its plaintive, unfinished song.

### The Flycatchers — Muscicapidae and Monarchidae
This group includes seven Australian robins, two fantails and five monarch flycatchers. None are related to European forms with the same common names.

**Scarlet Robin,** *Petroica multicolor.* The male bird has a brilliant red breast and a white patch above the beak. It prefers forested areas in the south-west.

**Red-capped Robin,** *P. goodenovii,* has a red patch above the beak. This is found throughout Western Australia, but is scarce in forested areas.

**Willy Wagtail,** *Rhipidura leucophrys.* A conspicuous pied bird which wags its tail side to side. It is often found around stock where it catches flies disturbed by the animals.

**Grey Fantail,** *R. fuliginosa,* readily approaches people, and spreads its wings and tail while climbing tree trunks to flush resting insects.

### The Thickheads — Pachycephalidae
These are relatively robust, large-headed birds which have loud, musical songs. They include five whistlers, three shrike-thrushes, the Crested Bell-bird and two shrike-tits.

**Crested Bell-bird,** *Oreoica gutturalis,* is a feature of the more arid areas where its haunting, ventriloquial, bell-like call can be heard.

**Golden Whistler,** *Pachycephala pectoralis,* is a familiar species with its piercing whistles. It is a bright yellow bird with a black head, and is found in the south-west, and eastern Australia.

### The Australian Chats — Ephthianuridae
A small family restricted to Australia. Four of the five known species occur in Western Australia.

**Crimson Chat,** *Ephthianura tricolor,* is a brilliantly coloured bird often seen near samphire and in mulga country.

**White-fronted Chat,** *Ephthianura albifrons,* is a white-fronted bird often seen walking on the ground in open areas or on samphire bushes in the southern half of Australia.

## The Sitellas and Tree-Creepers — Sittidae and Climacteridae

Sitellas are well known in Europe from the Nuthatch. Two species occur in the West, often flying around in small flocks. They have short tails and forage on tree trunks. Tree-creepers are larger, and not related to the European species. They also creep up tree trunks.

## The Flower-peckers — Dicaeidae

Mainly minute, colourful birds, this group includes the red Mistletoebird, that feeds on mistletoe berries, and five kinds of pardelote, which mainly feed on small insects on tree leaves.

## The White-eyes (Silvereyes) — Zosteropidae

Small green birds with a white border around their eyes. They are mainly fruit- and nectar-feeders.

**Western Silvereye, *Zosterops lateralis*.** This species often flies in flocks and may attack grapes during summers when Marri does not flower.

## The Honeyeaters — Meliphagidae

This family includes a number of species with curved bills, ranging in size from the small Brown Honeyeater to the raucous Red Wattlebird. There are 34 species in Western Australia.

**Singing Honeyeater, *Lichenostomus virescens*.** This is the most widespread and aggressive honeyeater. It sings in the early morning and has readily moved into urban habitats. Other urban species in the south-west are mainly Brown Honeyeaters and Red Wattlebirds.

**New Holland Honeyeater, *Phylidonyris novaehollandiae*,** has interesting social units which come together several times a day, cheeping noisily in the bushes. It is particularly abundant around banksias in the south-west.

**Red Wattlebird, *Anthochaera carunculata*,** is a large bird which visits flowers and continually makes raucous calls. It is found across the southern part of Australia.

## The Grass Finches — Spermestidae

These mainly live in open savannah country and have short, strong bills for feeding on grass seed. The exception is the Red-eared Firetail which lives in the forested south-west. Twelve species occur in Western Australia, including the Gouldian Finch, which is one of the most colourful species. Finches belonging to the Fringillidae do not occur here, apart from the introduced Goldfinch.

**Painted Firetail Finch, *Emblema pictum*,** is a strikingly crimson-coloured bird of spinifex country in the north-west. It prefers areas with rocky breakaways.

**Zebra Finch, *Taeniopygia guttata*,** is widely kept as a cagebird. It is often seen in large flocks around water and may be seen anywhere except in the extreme south-west.

**Double-bar Finch, *Taeniopygia bichenovii*,** is a white-fronted finch with black bars across the breast. It is a northern species extending as far as New South Wales.

## The Wood-swallows — Artamidae

These are somewhat swallow-like birds, although more robust. They frequently soar into the air and have pointed wing-tips. All five Australian species occur here.

## The Butcher-birds and Magpies — Cracticidae

Neither belongs to the family of the European birds with the same name. Butcher-birds derive their name from the habit off wedging prey in branches and magpies from their pied colouration. The Squeaker or Grey Currawong also belongs to this family.

**Pied Butcher-bird, *Cracticus nigrogularis*.** A handsome, black-headed bird which often settles on tall posts and dead branches. It has a very melodious, flute-like song.

**Western Magpie, *Gymnorhina dorsalis*.** These are large, aggressive birds which live in territorial groups. They have a melodious song. This species is restricted to the south-west corner, the rest of Western Australia being occupied by the Black-backed Magpie. The two species are distinguished by the female Western Magpie having white-bordered black feathers on her back.

## The Bowerbirds — Ptilonorhynchidae

Related to birds of paradise, these birds build bowers to attract females, where courtship and mating takes place. Ten species occur in Australia with two in Western Australia.

**Squeaker or Grey Currawong** (RIGHT)
**Australian Raven sunning itself** (BELOW)

**Spotted Bowerbird, *Chlamydera maculata*.** This is a large, brown bird found mainly on rocky hills, where rock figs grow in the north-west. The Great Bower-bird occurs in the Kimberley.

## *The Crows and Ravens — Corvidae*

This is the same family as the birds with the same names in other parts of the world. The five Australian species are all black; three occur in Western Australia.

**Pied Oystercatcher**

**Australian Raven, *Corvus coronoides*.** A large, glossy-black bird with conspicuous hackles around its throat when calling. Its characteristic call includes an ending which dies away in a macabre manner. It is restricted to the south-west, and occurs over much of eastern Australia. Outside the south-west corner there are two other species: the Australian Crow and Little Crow, which both lack the hackles and drawn-out ending to their calls.

# Reptiles & Amphibia

IN THE MOSTLY arid environment of Australia, reptiles have come to constitute one of the most important segments of the fauna. In some respects they have taken over the role of being the major small predators, which in other countries is usually mainly carried out by birds and small mammals. Western Australia has a rich fauna made up of about 12 turtles, 2 crocodiles, 130 skinks, 37 geckos, 19 snake-lizards, 42 dragons, 18 monitors and 102 snakes. Many of the Amphibia are also surprisingly well adapted to an arid environment, with over 70 species of frog being recorded. No salamanders or newts occur in Australia.

## The Crocodiles — Crocodylidae

The family includes alligators, caimans and the Gavial. Only crocodiles occur in Australia.

**Saltwater Crocodile, *Crocodylus porosus*.** This is one of the largest and most dangerous crocodiles. They will grow up to 7 m long, but only rarely exceed 5 m. Although preferring saltwater and estuarine conditions, they will travel long distances up flooded rivers. With crocodile numbers increasing, tourists in the north

**Green Turtle**

must be very cautious about where they swim.

**Freshwater Crocodile, *Crocodylus johnstoni*,** has a long, slender snout and prefers permanent freshwater. It will grow up to 3 m long and is harmless if treated with respect.

## The Turtles — Cheloniidae, Dermochelyidae and Chelidae

Several marine turtles are found along the northern coasts and freshwater species occur in rivers and lakes.

**Green Turtle, *Chelonia mydas*.** Although persecuted in most other parts of the world, these sea turtles have a healthy population around northern Australian coasts, stretching from Shark Bay to southern Queensland. They feed almost entirely on weed. The females come ashore on suitable beaches and lay about 100 eggs at a time. Conservation measures include fox control, because these animals dig up and destroy turtle eggs.

**Oblong Turtle, *Chelodina oblonga*.** This is the common species in the rivers and lakes of the south-west. It has a very long neck. Other species occur in the north.

## The Geckos — Gekkonidae

These are nocturnal lizards, some of which have special pads on their feet that allow them to climb glass windows and across ceilings. There are many ground-dwelling species, some living in rocks, others in leaf-litter or under bark.

**Barking Gecko, *Underwoodisaurus milii*.** A brightly coloured species which lives under rocks. It has an aggressive defense display involving standing high on its legs and barking. It is found in the south.

**Barking Gecko** (TOP)
**Knob-tailed Gecko** (BOTTOM)

**Knob-tailed Gecko, *Nephrurus levis*,** exhibits similar behaviour and lives in the north.

## The Dragon Lizards — Agamidae

These are fast-moving, long-legged lizards, often with a crest of scales. The frilled lizard from northern Australia is a well-known dragon lizard, occurring in the Kimberley region. Some species

**Thorny Devil** (ABOVE)
**Bobtail** (LEFT)

avoid the heat of day by climbing bushes, where the air temperature is lower than on the ground.

**Thorny Devil, *Moloch horridus*,** is an unmistakable lizard with its thorny scales. They feed on ants in the heat of the day, and rely on their thorny scales for protection from predators. They can only walk slowly, usually with their tail raised, and are found in most areas apart from Perth southward and in the Kimberley.

## The Monitor Lizards or Goannas — Varanidae

These are often large predatory lizards which can run at great speed. They include the largest lizard of all, the Komodo Dragon in Indonesia. Some are semi-aquatic, or arboreal.

**Gould's Goanna, *Varanus gouldii*,** grows up to about 1.6 m. This is the most widespread species, being found everywhere except in the extreme south-west. They usually have a white tip to the tail.

**Perentie, *V. giganteus*,** grows to more than 2.5 m long and has conspicuous transverse rows of spots. It is restricted to hot arid areas from the Pilbara to inland Queensland.

## The Snake-Lizards — Pygopodidae

These all have very reduced limbs and look like small snakes. They can often be found under stones and logs, or in dead grass trees.

**Burton's Snake-lizard, *Lialis burtonis*,** is a very fast, grey, snake-like animal up to about 35 cm long. It may be active in daylight or at night and feeds on small lizards. It can be found all over Australia, apart from the southern extremities.

## The Skinks — Skinkidae

This is a very successful group of lizards, which usually have smooth, shiny scales and sometimes reduced limbs. Many species burrow in loose sand; others can be seen climbing fence posts or tree trunks.

**Bobtail, *Tiliqua rugosa*.** This is an atypical skink with an unusual habit. It is slow moving and relies on its open-mouth, blue-tongue threat-display to ward off predators. The display must be effective, because it is still very common in the south-west, even in the presence of foxes. It is partly vegetarian, eating flowers, fruit and berries.

## The Snakes — Serpentes

The snakes of Western Australia include many different types, ranging from harmless blind worm-snakes and tree snakes, to some of the most venomous snakes in the world. There are also nine kinds of python, some of which may grow to as much as 4 m long.

**Stimpson's Python, *Morelia stimpsoni*.** A small species which grows up to 87 cm long. It ranges from Perth to Broome.

**Banded Cat-snake, *Boiga fusca*.** This is a tree-snake found in the Kimberley region. It grows up to 2 m long and is venomous, although probably not dangerous. It feeds on bats, lizards and birds.

**Jan's Banded Snake, *Vermicella bertholdi*.** An attractive snake which burrows in sand. It does not bite, and can be found in inland areas south of Exmouth.

**Tiger Snake, *Notonechis scutatus*.** One of the world's most deadly snakes. It often stands its ground instead of rushing off like the Dugite and other poisonous snakes. It may be active at night, seeking frogs in cool south-west swamps. It is usually black with an orange underbelly, and may grow to 1.2 m long.

Other deadly species include the Taipan in the Kimberley, and the Mulga Snake, Dugite and Gwardar elsewhere. Sea snakes and Death Adders are also deadly; the latter are particularly hazardous because of their sluggish behaviour and well-camouflaged bodies.

## The Frogs — Amphibia

Only two families of frogs occur in Western Australia — Hylidae and Leptodactylidae, although Microhylidae and Ranidae occur elsewhere in Australia. Many frogs have a burrowing habit, which is an important adaptation to living in arid environments. The Kimberley region has the richest variety of frogs, including many species which are not found in other parts of Western Australia. The introduced Cane-toad has not reached the Kimberley yet, although some have escaped in Perth from time to time.

### The Tree Frogs — Hylidae
This family includes frogs which have suckers on their toes so that they can stick onto leaves and vegetation. There are 72 Australian species with 26 recorded in Western Australia.

**Green Tree Frog, *Litoria caerulea*.** This is a large green frog which will climb high in the trees. It has a loud, deep, barking call, and has a northern distribution from Broome to New South Wales. A similar, more handsome species, *L. splendida*, which has a spotted pattern, is restricted to the Kimberley. Other Kimberley tree frogs include the Rocket Frog, *L. nasuta*, which is a prodigious leaper, and the small Roth's Tree Frog, *L. rothi*.

**Bull Frog, *L. moorei*.** A large tree-frog with green markings

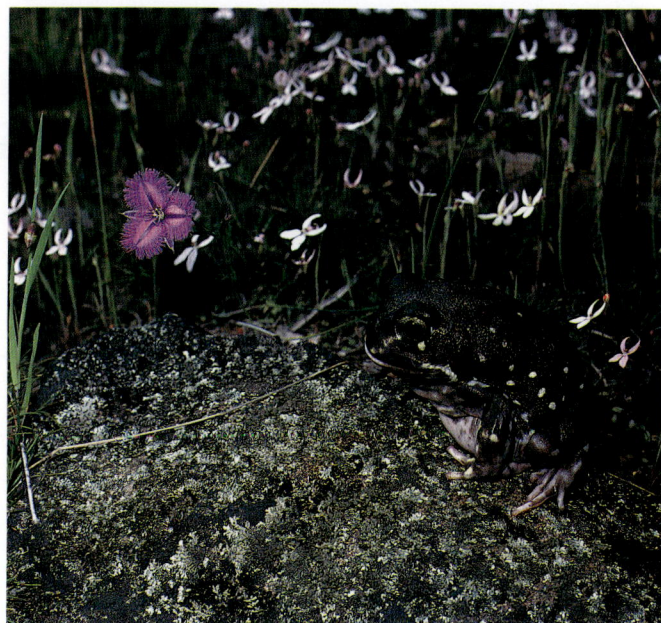

**White-spotted Frog** (ABOVE)
**Goldfields Frog** (LEFT)

found from Kalbarri to east of Albany. It rarely climbs above reed level, and mainly feeds on the ground. Its call is a soft, drawn-out growl. The closely related *L. cyclorhynchus* occurs near the south coast from Albany to Esperance. Also in the south-west is the smaller Slender Tree Frog, *L. adelaidensis*, which has a very loud, grating call.

### The Southern Frogs — Leptodactylidae
This family is confined to the Australian region, South Africa and the Americas. In Australia they include many ground-dwelling and burrowing species. There are 96 species in Australia with 44 in the West.

**White-spotted Frog, *Heleioporus albopunctatus*.** This is one of several burrowing frogs. The males dig holes in temporary swamps, from where they call before the winter rain falls. Females lay eggs in the burrows, and the male leaves when the burrows are flooded. The species used to be widespread in the Wheatbelt area, but most of its former haunts are now too saline.

**Goldfields Frog, *Neobatrachus wilsmorei*.** This is an arid zone frog found from the Pilbara to Kalgoorlie. It hunts at night, sitting with its head held high so that it can see potential prey. It breeds after summer rain.

**Turtle Frog, *Myobatrachus gouldii*,** is a strange-looking frog with a small head. It is rarely seen because it lives most of its life underground, feeding on termites. Breeding also takes place underground, where the tadpoles develop without an aquatic stage. It is restricted to the south-west.

# Insects

AUSTRALIA POSSESSES a very rich and diverse insect fauna. The few which are of economic or public health concern, and those which bite people or attack garden plants give the vast majority a bad name. Thousands of species exist which do not interact directly with human interests — many are attractive or have fascinating adaptations. Ants are particularly well-adapted to arid environments, so are very numerous, while butterflies, which do better in tropical rainforests, are comparatively poorly represented. The butterflies are surpassed in beauty by the rich variety of jewel beetles which are found here. Farming has unfortunately cleared much of the jewel beetle habitat, so many beetles have become rare or extinct. The beetles are now protected from collectors, but their habitat continues to be eroded by clearance and grazing.

## The Dragonflies and Damselflies — Odonata

This is a very ancient group of insects which in their day — the time before winged dinosaurs, birds and bats appeared — were the dominant winged predators. They form a prominent feature of the wildlife seen around pools, ponds, rivers and lakes. Bird-watchers often find themselves turning to dragonfly-watching when birds are not active. Being mainly dependent upon permanent water for breeding, many species are sedentary. The dragonfly fauna is mainly made up of three groups: southern species, northern species and itinerant species. The itinerant species are those which fly great distances and may be found anywhere. Over 300 species occur in Australia with 40 in the south-west, 34 in the Pilbara and about 60 in the Kimberley. The Pilbara region is particularly interesting in having varieties of

northern forms which have been isolated long enough for them to have evolved into unique species.

**Emperor Dragonfly, *Hemianax papuensis*.** This is the most widespread large dragonfly in Australia. Other itinerant species include the pale blue *Orthetrum caledonicum*, and small red *Diplacodes haematodes*.

**Millstream Damselfly, *Nososticta pilbara*,** breeds mainly in permanent flowing water associated with the aquifer in the area. It is distinct from a similar species which occurs in eastern Australia.

## The Cockroaches — Blattodea

Normally associated with the few introduced household pests, this family includes nearly 500 species in Australia. Some are attractively coloured, particularly species of *Polyzosteria*. These insects are well adapted to living in arid environments and have symbiotic micro-organisms which aid digestion of dry plant material.

## The Termites — Isoptera

This is a group closely allied to cockroaches which have become social insects. There are over 180 Australian species with many species in Western Australia. The group which builds fungus gardens, common in South-east Asia and Africa, does not occur here. *Coptotermes acinaciformis* is the main species which attacks wood in buildings. Others feed on dead leaves or grass, such as the Spinifex Termite, *Nasutitermes triodiae*.

## The Mantids — Mantodea

These predatory insects also appear to have come from cockroach

**Emperor Dragonfly** (LEFT)
**Large cockroach,** *Polyzosteria mitchelli* (BELOW)

**Large bushcricket (Tettigoniidae)** *(ABOVE)*
**Jewel Bug, *Coleotichus costatus*** *(ABOVE RIGHT)*
**Dragonfly-like Neuropteran (Ascalaphidae)** *(RIGHT)*

stock. There are many species which usually live on foliage and are hard to see except when they come to lights at night. Others inhabit the ground or live under stones.

## The Grasshoppers and Crickets — Orthoptera

Most of the chirping species belong to the crickets and bush-crickets, which have long antennae. The more diurnal grasshoppers have short antennae and include locusts. Few of these have any chirping calls, possibly because daytime calling attracts birds in Australia. Mole Crickets are common in damp places and along the sea shore where their tunnels are easy to find in the sand. Another group of burrowing species belongs to the Cylindrachetidae, which are only found in Australia, New Guinea and Patagonia. They are known as sandgropers.

## The Stick Insects — Phasmatodea

These are foliage-eating insects which are very hard to find. They include some large species which have sudden colourful displays to scare would-be predators.

## The Bugs and Cicadas — Hemiptera

This family includes an enormous range of insects with sucking mouthparts. They include scale insects, greenfly, waterskaters and a wide range of stink bugs. Cicadas have nymphs which live underground and suck juices from roots. Many species are found in the West, all of which have distinctive calls. The bugs are somewhat beetle-like and include Crusader Bugs and the attractive Jewel Bug, *Coleotichus costatus*, which lives on *Acacia cyclops*.

## The Antlions and Lacewings — Neuroptera

Antlions are particularly well adapted to dry environments, because their pit-fall traps make use of dry sand. The larva waits at the base and throws sand at ants falling in the trap until it can grab hold of them. The adults are dragonfly-like insects, which are often attracted to lights at night.

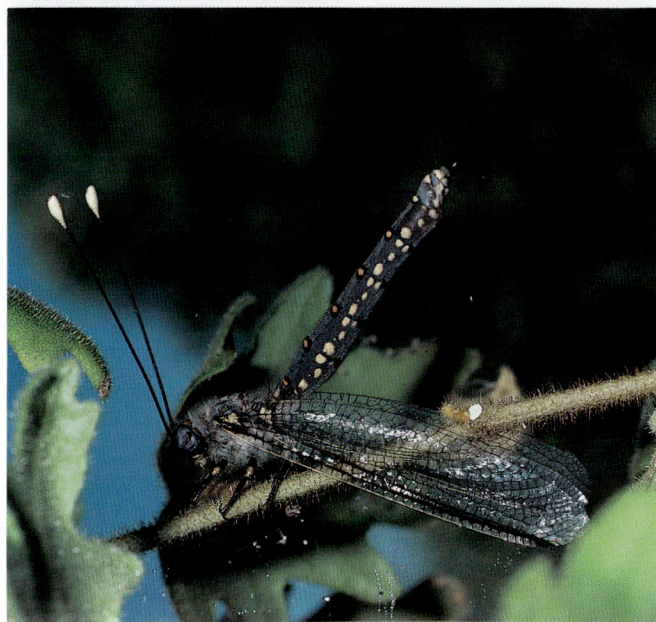

## The Beetles — Coleoptera

A huge range of beetles is found in Western Australia. The order is so large that many are still undescribed. They include the beautiful jewel beetles (Buprestidae) which have larvae that feed in the roots of trees or in the stems of plants. The adults are fast flying and active in sunlight, visiting flowers. Other beetles include stag beetles (Lucanidae) in the south-west and the extraordinary pie-dish beetles (Tenebrionidae), which frequent arid areas.

## The Flies — Diptera

This order is mainly associated with such insects as bushflies, houseflies and mosquitoes, but includes an enormous range of attractive or inconspicuous insects. Mosquitoes can occur in enormous numbers after rain in arid areas, and in places subject to flooding in the south-west. Some can transmit diseases such as Ross River Virus and MVE, which normally attack birds or large marsupials, but also can cause serious illness in people. Campers are advised to cover up and use repellents when biting mosquitoes are particularly numerous. Malaria could be carried by mosquitoes here if the parasite was introduced by infected people. Attractive flies include hoverflies (Syrphidae), beeflies (Bombyliidae), and robberflies (Asilidae). Other large flies include a variety of horseflies (Tabanidae — known locally as March or Marsh flies).

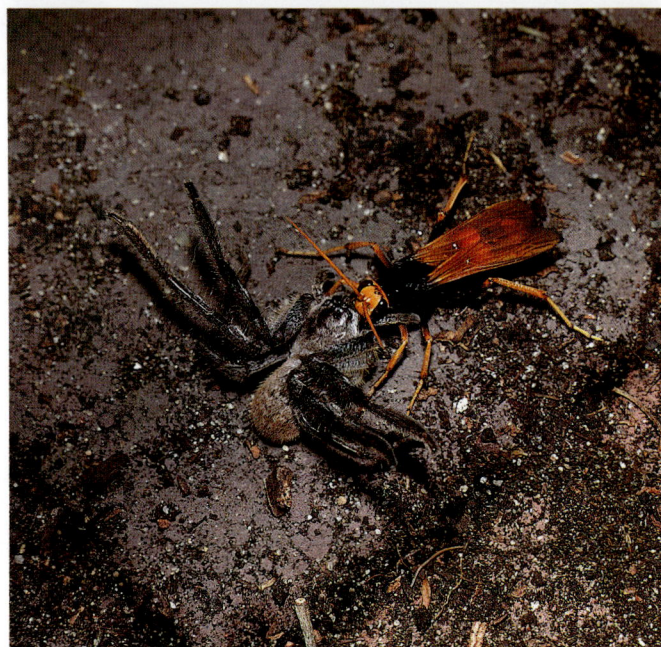

**Hornet-like robberfly (Asilidae) with large wasp** *(TOP LEFT)*
**Gum Emperor Moth caterpillar, *Antheraea helena*** *(TOP RIGHT)*
**Spider-hunting wasp with huntsman spider** *(LEFT)*
**Inch ant, also known as a bulldog ant** *(ABOVE)*
**Wanderer butterfly** *(OPPOSITE)*

## The Butterflies and Moths — Lepidoptera

One of the main features of this group is that they have scales on their wings, which renders them difficult to catch or hold, and they can fall unharmed out of spiders' webs. Their early stages are in the form of caterpillars, like the witchety grubs eaten by Aborigines. These are the larvae of huge moths (Cossidae), and feed mainly on the roots of wattles. In the south-west Gum Emperor Moth caterpillars can be found on Marri trees, and the moths fly in September. The butterflies include the migratory Australian Painted-lady, *Vanessa kershawi*, which is very similar to the species found in other parts of the world, also the Australian Admiral, *V. itea*, which has caterpillars that feed on nettles and other plants in the Urticaceae. The Wanderer, *Danaus plexippus*, is probably the most conspicuous butterfly. It is a migratory species which island-hopped across the Pacific from its native America,

arriving here in 1870. The Cabbage White, *Pieris rapae*, is another common non-native species. Its caterpillars feed on nasturtiums as well as cabbages.

## The Ants, Bees and Wasps — Hymenoptera

This is another group which has an enormous variety of species. It includes the sawflies whose gum-leaf eating larvae are known as spitfires (Pergidae), and ichneumons, which lay eggs in caterpillars and are also responsible for pollinating slipper orchids. The bees include Dawson's Bee, *Amegilla dawsoni*, which is a large bee that nests communally, often along outback roads. The bees noisily buzz passers-by, but do not sting unless caught. Wasps include many spider-hunting species, some of which may catch large huntsman spiders and take them to their holes. The social species include species of paper wasps, *Polistes*. Ants are ubiquitous, especially the Meat Ant, *Iridomyrmex purpureus*. These have large nests with many holes on open ground, and bite anyone who approaches. Bulldog, or inch ants, *Myrmecia*, are interesting because they have primitive, wasp-like characteristics, the ants having evolved from wasp-like ancestors. They include large black species and rusty red ones, which have stings like wasps. Non-native Hymenoptera include the Honeybee, Argentine Ant and, in Perth, the European Wasp, *Vespula germanica*.

# Scorpions, Spiders, Snails & Other terrestrial invertebrates

## The Scorpions — Scorpionida

Scorpions belong to a very ancient group — the tracks of their distant ancestors, sea scorpions, can be seen in Devonian rocks at Kalbarri. Scorpions may be found anywhere in Western Australia, usually living in holes or under stones, while some small ones are more often found under bark on dead trees. The smaller ones often have a more painful sting than the larger kinds, but none are dangerous. Seventeen species have been recorded here.

**Urodacus novaehollandiae,** is the larger, dark-coloured species commonly found in the south-west. It digs oval holes, often under stones or logs, and only comes out during the warmer parts of the year when its insect prey is active, especially on hot summer nights.

**U. hartmeyer,** is a large, pale species which lives along the coast from Perth to Exmouth, where it often digs holes in sand dunes.

## The Spiders — Araneae

This is a remarkable group which sprang from the same stock as scorpions and ticks, and had already developed the web-building habit by the Cretaceous. Western Australia has a fascinating range of spiders, including many which have painful or even dangerous bites, so they should be treated with respect. Fortunately only a few species live in places where they are likely to bite people. The Redback, *Lactrodectus hasselti* (Theridiidae), is one of these. It is common in gardens, living under pots and garden furniture where people are likely to unknowingly put their fingers on it. It is a close relative of the Black Widow, and is thought to be a recent im-

migrant into Australia. Other dangerous species include trap-door spiders (Mygalomorphs) and some of the larger wolf spiders (Lycosidae), which need highly toxic bites to kill large insects or even geckos. *Missulena occatoria* is an unusual trap-door spider in that the male can often be seen walking over the ground in the daytime looking for females.

## The Orb-weaving Spiders —Argiopidae

**Golden-orb Spiders, *Nephila*,** are very large spiders which build huge webs between trees, adding conspicuous patches of debris so that birds do not blunder into them.

***Argiope*** builds orb-webs and has a tiger-striped body.

**Christmas Spiders, *Gasteracantha minax*,** have star-like spikes on their bodies, and live in communal webs, mainly built late in the year.

## The Jumping Spiders — Salticidae
These spiders do not build webs, but catch prey by jumping on them. Some, like the Peacock Spiders, *Maratus*, are brightly coloured.

## The Huntsmen Spiders — Sparassidae.
The large *Isopoda* have long hairy legs and often live under bark, coming out at night. They can bite, but are relatively harmless.

**Large Scorpion, *Urodacus hartmeyeri* (BELOW LEFT)**
**Redback Spider (BELOW)**

Trap-door Spider, *Missulena occatoria* (RIGHT)
Centipede, *Scolopendra morsitans* (ABOVE)

## The Ticks and Mites — Acarina

Ticks can usually be found on Bobtail Lizards and bushwalkers often have tick bites. Ticks attack most of the larger animals, requiring a blood meal for each stage of their development. The eggs usually hatch after damp weather in March-April, when large numbers of tiny ticks can be picked up off the vegetation, especially near where kangaroos rest. The adults are active in late spring, and may walk at great speed towards potential hosts. Bites are very irritating and may last for weeks. Insect repellents are an effective deterrent.

## The Centipedes —Chilopoda

Large centipedes are commonly found, and have painful bites. *Cormocephalus aurantiipes* may be found under stones in the Jarrah forest and *Scolopendra morsitans* in more arid areas. Some species living in arid areas dig slit-like holes which look somewhat like scorpion holes.

## The Millipedes — Diplopoda

Millipedes are normally shiny cylindrical animals which stain hands with foul-smelling oil. However, in the Pilbara there is a very interesting millipede which is social. This is the Pincushion Millipede, *Unixenus mjobergi*. It is a tiny animal, but lives in enormous groups which march along like ants, often near rivers. They may invade buildings and caravans. It is also known in India.

## Peripatus — Onychophora

*Peripatoides gilesii* is an unusual animal thought to be evolved from the stock which also gave rise to the insects. They are harmless, but can defend themselves by firing a volley of sticky threads over assailants. They can be found under stones and damp logs in winter in the south-west.

## Other Terrestrial Invertebrates

In this primarily arid environment, slugs and snails are not abundant. The white snail shells often found in mallee areas belong to species of *Bothriembryon*. Most others seen belong to the introduced Mediterranean and Garden Snails. Other interesting invertebrates include a species of terrestrial nemertine worm, *Geonemertes* (most Nemertea are marine), and *Geoplana* which is a terrestrial flatworm (Turbellaria). The largest earthworms in Western Australia, *Megascolex imparycistis*, grow up to 30 cm long and live near Lancelin.

# *Aquatic Life*

## Freshwater

The south-west has an interesting array of aquatic animals. They include many crustaceans, especially freshwater crayfish. Five species are found, the best known being the Marron, *Cherax tenuimanus*, which is one of the largest species in the world. Fish include the minnow-like *Galaxias*, Pygmy Perch and Nightfish. Freshwater mussels, *Westralunio carteri*, can be found in rivers and there are many aquatic insects including dragonflies, mayflies, alderflies and caddisflies. The Crustacea include the strange Phreatoicids which are slaters (*Isopods*) that are flattened laterally so that they look like Gammarid shrimps (*Amphipods*). Temporary waters inland often have fairy shrimps (*Branchinella*) and tadpole shrimps (*Triops*). The introduced Brine Shrimp, *Artemia salina*, lives in salt lakes on Rottnest Island.

Northern rivers have many species of fish including kinds of hardyhead and grunter. Archer Fish can be found in the Kimberley — these fish squirt drops of water at insects on overhanging vegetation. Caves in the Cape Range area have Blind Cave-eels.

## Saltwater and Marine

The marine and estuarine environment offers a great variety of habitats from mangrove swamp to coral reefs, and warm tropical waters to cool temperate conditions. Northern sandy beaches have large numbers of ghost crabs, which are mainly active at night. One species occurs on Rottnest Island. In more sheltered areas one can see Fiddler Crabs and Mudskippers — little fish which hop over mud in mangrove swamps.

Ningaloo Reef in the north-west has a very rich and diverse coral reef fauna. There are large clams, bailer shells and cowries; also many corals, colourful reef fish and coral shrimps. Large anemones have anemone fish, and anemone shrimps which live amongst the stinging tentacles. During hot summer days many rays and small sharks come close to the beaches to bask in the warm water, while off the coast the largest shark in the world is commonly found — the harmless Whale Shark. Stinging animals, sometimes dangerous, include the Stonefish, Blue-ringed Octopus and cone shells.

**Ghost Crab**

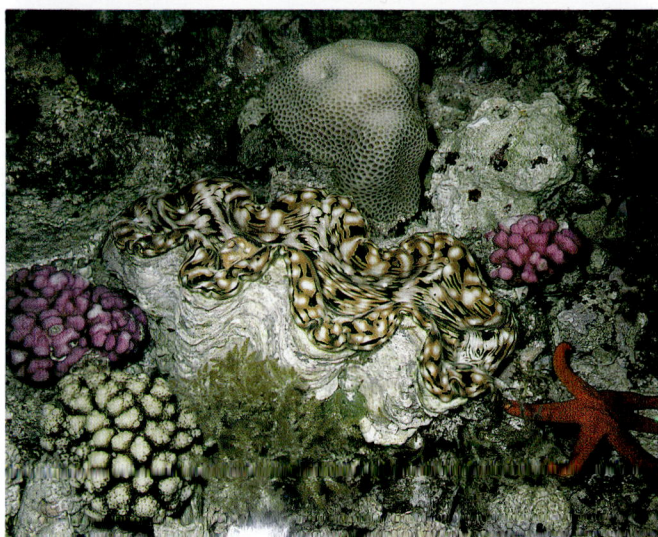

**Clam,** *Tridacna (RIGHT)*
**Anemone fish. This is a Two-spot Damselfish which lives in anemones when small** *(ABOVE)*
**Blue-ringed Octopus** *(ABOVE RIGHT)*

Further north, especially along the Kimberley coast, swimming in summer is hazardous with box jellyfish, sea snakes, sharks and stingrays. Crocodiles are always a hazard — Barramundi fishermen beware! In the cooler southern waters there are many rock crabs, limpets and periwinkles on rocky shores. Cuttlefish, porcupine fish and sea horses live in the beds of sea grass. Large shoals of Australian Salmon approach the shore and Sun Fish (*Mola mola*) can sometimes be seen, especially near Esperance. Winter storms bring many bluebottle jellyfish, and By-the-wind Sailor (*Velella*) onto the beaches. Stinging animals include Cobbler, which is a catfish, and the dangerous Blue-ringed Octopus.

Rock lobsters are an important feature of the West Australian coast, and support an extensive industry. The fishery is strictly managed to avoid overfishing.

# *Further Reading*

**Beard, J. S.** *Plant Life of Western Australia*. Kangaroo Press, 1990.
**Bennett, E. M.** *The Bushland Plants of Kings Park Western Australia*. Kings Park, 1988.
**Blombery, A. M.** *The Living Centre of Australia*. Kangaroo Press, 1985.
**Ericson, R. et al.** *Flowers and Plants of Western Australia*. A. H. & A. W. Reed, 1973.
**Hoffman, N. & A. Brown** *Orchids of South-West Australia*. University of W. A. Press, 1984.
**Marchant, N. G. et al.** *Flora of the Perth Region. Parts one and two*. Western Australian Herbarium, 1987.
**Mitchell, A. A. & D. G. Wilcox** *Plants of the Arid Shrublands of Western Australia*. University of W.A. Press, 1988.
**Sharr, F. A.** *Western Australian plant names and their meanings*. A glossary. University of W.A. Press, 1978 reprinted 1988.
**Storr, G. M. & R. E. Johnstone** *A Field Guide to the Birds of Western Australia*. W.A. Museum, 2nd Edition 1985.
**Strahan, R.** *Complete Book of Australian Mammals*. Angus and Robertson, 1983.
**Taylor, J. C.** *Evolution in the Outback*. Kangaroo Press, 1987.
**Taylor, J. C.** *Flower Power. Fascinating interrelationships between insects and plants*. Kangaroo Press, 1989.
**Taylor, J. C.** *Australia's Southwest and Our Future*. Kangaroo Press, 1990.
**W.A. Museum** Guides to Inland Fishes, Regional Birds, Frogs, Snakes, Dragons, Skinks etc.

# Index & Glossary

# MAP 2

# THE NORTHWEST

N

## NATIONAL PARKS
14  Kalbarri
15  Cape Range
16  Karijini (Hamersley Range)
17  Millstream-Chichester
18  Collier Range
19  Rudall River

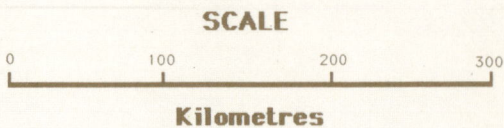

## SCALE

0        100        200        300

**Kilometres**

Port Hedland

De G

*Burrup Peninsula*

Karratha

Ma

*Barrow Island*

*Chichester Ra.*

17

*Fortescue R.*

16

Onslow

Exmouth

*Hamersley Ra.*

15

*Cape Ra.*

*Ningaloo Reef*

Paraburdoo

*Ashburton R.*

Coral Bay

18

*Kennedy Ra.*

*Lyons R.*

Mt Augustus

*Gascoyne R.*

Carnarvon

Gascoyne Junction

*Bernier & Dorre Is.*

*Shark Bay*

Monkey
Mia

Meekatharra

*Hamelin Pool*

Useless Loop

*Murchison R.*

*Zuytdorp Cliffs*

Cue

Kalbarri

14

Galena

Mt Magnet